WORLD
HISTORY SERIES

The Hundred
Years' War

by
William W. Lace

Lucent Books, P.O. Box 289011, San Diego, CA 92198-9011

Titles in the World History Series

The Age of Feudalism	The Hundred Years' War
Ancient Greece	The Roman Empire
The French and Indian War	The Roman Republic
Hitler's Reich	The Russian Revolution

Library of Congress Cataloging-in-Publication Data

Lace, William W.
    The Hundred Years' War / by William W. Lace.
        p.   cm.—(World history series)
    Includes bibliographical references and index.
    Summary: Describes the conflict between France and England known as the Hundred Years War and explains how its results were felt everywhere in Europe.
    ISBN 1-56006-233-9 (acid-free paper)
    1. Hundred Years' War, 1339–1453—Juvenile literature.
[1. Hundred Years' War 1339–1453.]   I. Title.   II. Series.
DC96.L33   1994
944'.025—dc20

                                                93-22871
                                                CIP
                                                AC

Contents

Foreword

Each year on the first day of school, nearly every history teacher faces the task of explaining why his or her students should study history. One logical answer to this question is that exploring what happened in our past explains how the things we often take for granted—our customs, ideas, and institutions—came to be. As statesman and historian Winston Churchill put it, "Every nation or group of nations has its own tale to tell. Knowledge of the trials and struggles is necessary to all who would comprehend the problems, perils, challenges, and opportunities which confront us today." Thus, a study of history puts modern ideas and institutions in perspective. For example, though the founders of the United States were talented and creative thinkers, they clearly did not invent the concept of democracy. Instead, they adapted some democratic ideas that had originated in ancient Greece and with which the Romans, the British, and others had experimented. An exploration of these cultures, then, reveals their very real connection to us through institutions that continue to shape our daily lives.

Another reason often given for studying history is the idea that lessons exist in the past from which contemporary societies can benefit and learn. This idea, although controversial, has always been an intriguing one for historians. Those that agree that society can benefit from the past often quote philosopher George Santayana's famous statement, "Those who cannot remember the past are condemned to repeat it." Historians who ascribe to Santayana's philosophy believe that, for

example, studying the events that led up to the major world wars or other significant historical events would allow society to chart a different and more favorable course in the future.

Just as difficult as convincing students to realize the importance of studying history is the search for useful and interesting supplementary materials that present historical events in a context that can be easily understood. The volumes in Lucent Books' World History Series attempt to present a broad, balanced, and penetrating view of the march of history. Ancient Egypt's important wars and rulers, for example, are presented against the rich and colorful backdrop of Egyptian religious, social, and cultural developments. The series engages the reader by enhancing historical events with these cultural contexts. For example, in *Ancient Greece,* the text covers the role of women in that society. Slavery is discussed in *The Roman Empire,* as well as how slaves earned their freedom. The numerous and varied aspects of everyday life in these and other societies are explored in each volume of the series. Additionally, the series covers the major political, cultural, and philosophical ideas as the torch of civilization is passed from ancient Mesopotamia and Egypt, through Greece, Rome, Medieval Europe, and other world cultures, to the modern day.

The material in the series is formatted in a thorough, precise, and organized manner. Each volume offers the reader a comprehensive and clearly written overview of an important historical event or period. The topic under discussion is placed in a broad, historical context. For example, *The Italian Renaissance* begins with a discussion of the High Middle Ages and the loss of central control that allowed certain Italian cities to develop artistically. The book ends by looking forward to the Reformation and interpreting the societal changes that grew out of the Renaissance. Thus, students are not only involved in an historical era, but also enveloped by the events leading up to that era and the events following it.

One important and unique feature in the World History Series is the primary and secondary source quotations that richly supplement each volume. These quotes are useful in a number of ways. First, they allow students access to sources they would not normally be exposed to because of the difficulty and obscurity of the original source. The quotations range from interesting anecdotes to far-sighted cultural perspectives and are drawn from historical witnesses both past and present. Second, the quotes demonstrate how and where historians themselves derive their information on the past as they strive to reach a consensus on historical events. Lastly, all of the quotes are footnoted, familiarizing students with the citation process and allowing them to verify quotes and/or look up the original source if the quote piques their interest.

Finally, the books in the World History Series provide a detailed launching point for further research. Each book contains a bibliography specifically geared toward student research. A second, annotated bibliography introduces students to all the sources the author consulted when compiling the book. A chronology of important dates gives students an overview, at a glance, of the topic covered. Where applicable, a glossary of terms is included.

In short, the series is designed not only to acquaint readers with the basics of history, but also to make them aware that their lives are a part of an ongoing human saga. Perhaps they will then come to the same realization as famed historian Arnold Toynbee. In his monumental work, *A Study of History,* he wrote about becoming aware of history flowing through him in a mighty current, and of his own life "welling like a wave in the flow of this vast tide."

Important Dates in the Hundred Years' War

A.D. 1310　　1320　　　1330　　　1340　　　1340　　　1340　　　1370　　　1380

1312
Birth of Prince Edward of Windsor, son of King Edward II and Queen Isabella.

1327
Edward II is deposed and murdered; Prince Edward becomes King Edward III of England.

1328
Charles IV of France dies without an heir; Philip of Valois becomes King Philip VI of France; marriage of Edward III and Philippa of Hainault.

1330
Edward III overthrows Mortimer and imprisons Queen Isabella; birth of Edward of Woodstock.

1334
Edward III defeats the Scots at Halidon Hill.

1336
Philip VI moves fleet to the English Channel; Robert of Artois takes refuge in England.

1337
Philip VI declares that Edward III has forfeited Guyenne; Edward sends Philip a letter of defiance; beginning of the Hundred Years' War.

1339
Edward III's first attack on France.

1340
Edward III declares himself king of France; English fleet defeats the French at Sluys.

1342
Edward III leads troops to Brittany.

1346
English defeat French at Battle of Crécy.

1347
Edward III captures Calais.

1348–1350
The Black Death ravages Europe.

1350
Philip VI dies; John II becomes king of France.

1356
English, under the Black Prince, defeat the French at Poitiers; King John II is captured and imprisoned in England.

1358
King John's son, Charles, is driven from Paris by rioters; revolt of the Jacquerie.

1360
Treaty of Brétigny surrenders much of France to Edward III.

1364
John II dies; Charles V becomes king of France.

1367
The Black Prince defeats forces led by Bertrand du Guesclin at Nájera, Spain.

1369
Charles V declares England's forfeiture of Guyenne; war in France resumes.

1374
England loses all lands in France except Guyenne and Calais.

1376
The Black Prince dies.

1377
Edward III dies; Richard II becomes king of England.

1380
Death of Guesclin; death of Charles V; Charles VI becomes king of France.

1381
Peasants' Revolt in England.

1389
Truce of Leulinghen between French and English.

1392
King Charles VI of France goes insane.

1390	1400	1410	1420	1430	1440	1450	1460

1394
Marriage of Richard II and Isabella, daughter of Charles VI.

1399
Richard II is deposed; Henry IV becomes king of England,

1407
The duke of Orléans is murdered in Paris by agents of John the Fearless of Burgundy.

1411
Henry IV sends troops to France to help John the Fearless against the Armagnacs.

1413
Henry IV dies; Henry V becomes king of England.

1415
Henry V invades France; English defeat French at Agincourt.

1419
John the Fearless is murdered by the Armagnacs.

1420
Treaty of Troyes; English occupy Paris.

1422
Henry V and Charles VI die; Henry VI becomes king of England and is recognized north of the Loire River as King Henri II of France.

1423
English defeat the dauphinists at Cravant.

1424
English defeat the dauphinists at Verneuil.

1428
English begin siege of Orléans; Joan of Arc appears before Charles VII.

1429
Joan of Arc relieves Orléans; Charles VII is crowned at Reims; Joan fails to recapture Paris.

1430
Joan of Arc is captured by Burgundians.

1431
Joan of Arc is burned at the stake at Rouen; Henry VI of England is crowned Henri II in Paris.

1435
The duke of Bedford dies; Treaty of Arras between Charles VII and Duke Philip of Burgundy.

1436
Paris is recaptured by French.

1444
Truce of Tours between France and England.

1445
Marriage of Henry VI and Margaret of Anjou.

1448
England surrenders Le Maine to France.

1449
Charles VII attacks Normandy.

1450
Normandy becomes French after English are defeated at Battle of Fromigny.

1451
France conquers Guyenne.

1452
English, under Sir John Talbot, reoccupy Guyenne.

1453
Talbot is defeated and killed at Battle of Castillon; English leave Guyenne; end of the Hundred Years' War.

1455
War of the Roses begins in England with the Battle of St. Albans.

The Endless War

The Hundred Years' War began in 1337, but the chain of events that caused it started centuries earlier. In 1066 a daring French duke, William of Normandy, led a small army to England. Against heavy odds he defeated the English and made himself king. He thus became, at the same time, king of England and a duke in France.

This was possible under the system known as feudalism.

Feudalism was an economic, social, and military system developed in the Middle Ages, the period of time that began after the fall of the Roman Empire and lasted until about 1300. Under feudalism members of the upper classes were

A medieval feudal estate usually included a lord's castle surrounded by land that was cultivated by serfs—peasants who received shelter and protection from the lord in return for working the land.

granted lands (fiefs) by higher ranking nobles in return for military service. The person receiving a fief, called a vassal, under-
went a ceremony. He knelt before the
overlord—the person granting him the
land—placed his hands between those of
the overlord, and swore an oath of
homage to be faithful to his overlord and
to fight on his side if needed. The overlord, in exchange, agreed to give protection to the vassal.

Feudal society had several layers. An
ordinary knight might be the vassal of a
baron, who was the vassal of a count, who
was the vassal of a duke, who was the vassal
of the king. The titles of the nobility varied
from place to place, but the system remained essentially the same.

A person might hold different lands
from two or more overlords. These overlords might be at war with one another.
The vassal could not fight on both sides at
once, so a system was used whereby a vassal
could give full homage to only one lord
and a form of limited homage to any others.

Personal Loyalty

*King Henry II of England was also the count of
Aquitaine and duke of Anjou, two regions in
France. All of these lands were known as the
Angevin Empire.*

Under feudalism individual loyalty was
pledged to another individual and not to a
nation. Patriotism, loyalty to one's country,
simply did not exist. Countries as we know
them did not exist. Then a country was
made up of the territory controlled by a
king and his vassals. Borders were not
fixed and frequently changed as a result of
war and shifting alliances. A knight might
consider himself a subject of the king of
France but not a citizen of France.

Thus, William of Normandy, known to
history as the Conqueror, was both a vassal

and a king—a vassal by birth and a king by
conquest. Soon after the conquest William
rewarded his followers, who already held
lands in France, with additional lands in
England. That made them vassals of both
King William of England and, through
William as duke of Normandy, of the king
of France. This arrangement worked as
long as the interests of the kings of England
and France did not conflict.

Such a conflict, however, did arise a
century after William. Henry II, a great-
grandson of William, came to the throne

of England in 1154. His father was Geoffrey, count of Anjou in France, whose family name was Plantagenet, for a flower he wore in his hat. Upon Geoffrey's death Henry became count. Later, through marriage, he also became count of Aquitaine, a large territory in southwestern France. Henry thus ruled not only England, but also a third of France.

The Angevin Empire

Henry's lands, stretching from Scotland to Spain, were known as the Angevin (from Anjou) Empire, and Henry was the first in a long line of Plantagenet kings of England. He constantly attempted to add to his empire, usually at the expense of France. He was far more powerful than the king of France, to whom he was formally a vassal.

Tension between England and France grew as fighting occurred between Angevin and French territories. It also became the policy of each to give help to the other's enemies. For example, France was an ally of and aided Scotland, which was constantly in revolt against England. England, which depended heavily on exporting wool, was an ally of and aided the cloth merchants of Flanders, who periodically tried to shake off the rule of their French counts.

The Angevin Empire did not last long after Henry's death in 1189. Most of it was lost by Henry II's son, John (the same Prince John of the Robin Hood legends). Eventually, all that remained in France of the Angevin Empire were Guyenne (a strip of land 150 miles long and 50 miles wide along the southwestern coast)

The feudal system made it possible for Henry II to rule Scotland, England, Wales, and much of France. After Henry's death in 1189, however, his son John, lost control of most of these lands.

and the small county of Ponthieu. Even so, the dual role of the kings of England as vassals of the kings of France continued to cause endless trouble and was a prime cause of the Hundred Years' War.

Royal Crisis in France

Finally, in 1328, a series of deaths in the French royal family brought about a crisis. The king of England, Edward III, claimed the throne of France. His claim was refused, and the Hundred Years' War began. Historian David Douglas wrote, however, that France and England

had been brought into an intimate historical relationship from which neither could escape. Of this relationship, close, embarrassing, and enduring, the Hundred Years War was at once a symptom and a solvent. This was a feudal world, and in its complicated meshes both countries were in-

volved. It is easy—and it is just—to discover the immediate cause of the outbreak of the Hundred Years War in the impossible situation created by the position of an English king [Edward III] who was also duke of Gascony [Guyenne]. As an independent prince, he was also a French vassal, subject in France to a monarch whose interests were frequently directly opposed to his own. Here, indeed, was a reason for war much more important than Edward III's much advertised claim to the French throne.[1]

The war actually lasted more than one hundred years—from 1337 to 1453—but fighting was not continuous. There were numerous truces, one lasting almost twenty-five years.

It was a time of great contrasts. Knights in shining armor performed brave deeds. Minstrels sang their praises, and fair ladies looked on. At the same time, the lives of the common people, most of whom already lived in wretched conditions, grew even worse. At various times during the war they were hunted down and killed like animals, tortured, and robbed. It was a time of great piety, during which soldiers devoutly prayed for God's protection. Yet those same soldiers might rape and slaughter the women and children of a captured town.

The Hundred Years' War was also a time of tremendous change. Not everything during the hundred years was a result of the war, but its results were felt everywhere within the two kingdoms and throughout Europe. For more than a century France and England were locked in a seemingly endless war. As historian Edouard Perroy wrote, "Around them, the world became transformed."[2]

King Edward III of England claimed the right to the French throne in 1328. His claim started the Hundred Years' War, though some historians blame feudalism itself, which let an English king also be a French duke.

1 Plantagenet and Valois

Edward II was one of the worst kings in the history of England. He was tall, fair, and strong, like most of the Plantagenets, but had no ability to rule. He had almost no willpower of his own and was controlled by others. He reigned from 1307 to 1327, and for most of that time England was in a state of civil war. On one side were the leading nobles. On the other was Edward, under the complete domination, initially, of court favorites and, later, of his wife.

King Edward II was one of England's worst kings. His rule was weak, and he was completely dominated by his wife, Isabella, who plotted to usurp the throne.

Edward II's wife was Isabella, daughter of King Philip the Fair of France. After the birth of her son Edward in 1312, Isabella began plotting to have her husband removed from the throne and to rule England through her son.

After the death of Isabella's father, the French crown went in turn to her three brothers (Louis X, Philip the Long, and Charles IV), each of whom died after short reigns. Each of these kings tried to get Edward II to go to France to swear the oath of homage for the territory of Guyenne. Edward always came up with excuses not to go. It was humiliating for a king to humble himself before a fellow sovereign, and the kings of England repeatedly did all they could to avoid the ceremony.

Finally, in 1325, Edward II sent his son to do homage in his place before Charles IV. The twelve-year-old boy was accompanied by Isabella and her lover, Roger de Mortimer, earl of March. Isabella lived so openly with Mortimer that Charles IV, shocked, banished her from France.

After Edward completed his task, Isabella took the three to the small county of Hainault (in modern-day Belgium) instead of returning to England. There, she and Mortimer plotted a rebellion against Edward II and enlisted the help

A Medieval Contract

"The said Richard is retained and attached to the same king and duke for peace and war for the term of his life in the following manner, that is, that the aforesaid Richard shall be bound to serve the aforesaid king and duke as well in time of peace as of war for the duration of his life and to work with him in what areas the said king and duke shall please, along with two companions, men-at-arms and six archers, well and conveniently arrayed for war. And the said Richard shall be entitled to wages and bouche [an allowance for food] of court in the various places to which he shall be sent by the letters of the aforesaid king and duke, by his commandment. And the same Richard will take from the said king and duke for himself, his aforesaid companions, men-at-arms, and aforesaid archers the customary wages of war as the aforesaid king and duke will take from our lord the king for similar men-at-arms and archers, at the hands of the treasurer of the same king and duke for the war that shall be waged at the time. And with regard to the horses of the said Richard and his said companions, men-at-arms, taken and lost in war in the service of the aforesaid king and duke, together with the equipment of himself, his said companions, men-at-arms, archers abovenamed, their horses, servants, and harness whatsoever and also from the beginning of this year of war, and for the prisoners of war, profits of war, taken or gained by the said Richard, his companions, men-at-arms, and archers abovenamed, or for any of their people and servants, the said king and duke will act towards the same Richard in the same way as he will do to other esquires of his estate and condition for similar men-at-arms and archers, as is above said."

Isabella, queen of England, despised her husband, Edward II. With the help of her lover, she overthrew him and had her son crowned King Edward III.

A New Line of Kings

In 1328 Charles IV, the last of Isabella's brothers, died. The French were grim as they buried their monarch. For three hundred years the Capetian kings, descendants of Hugh Capet, had followed one another, father to son, onto the throne. Charles IV, latest in this line, died without having a son, but his wife, Jeanne, was pregnant. In April she gave birth to a stillborn daughter, and the line came to an end.

A council of the leading nobles of France had named Charles's cousin, Philip of Valois, to act as regent, or governor, in case a boy was born. Now, Philip took the throne for himself. He called together the Estates, an assembly of nobles, churchmen, and lawyers, who proclaimed him Philip VI. Historian Desmond Seward wrote: "They did not know how much misery and destruction they had thereby brought upon France."[4]

One objection was raised. Two English ambassadors argued that the throne of France should go to Queen Isabella of England, since she was Philip the Fair's daughter, or to Isabella's son, Edward III. Edward III, they reasoned, was Philip the Fair's grandson, while Philip of Valois was only a nephew. The Estates would not allow it. Jean Froissart, later employed as a clerk by Edward III's queen, Philippa, wrote:

> After the death of the last of them [Isabella's brothers], the twelve peers [dukes] and the barons of France would not give the crown to their sister who was Queen of England; for they held and maintained, and still do, that the kingdom of France is so noble that it cannot go or descend to a woman, or

of Hainault's count, William. There, also, the young Edward saw and fell in love with William's twelve-year-old daughter, Philippa. They married two years later. Philippa bore five children in her first eight years of marriage to Edward, the first of whom was the heir to the throne, Edward of Woodstock, born in 1330.

In 1327, with the help of William of Hainault's troops, Isabella and Mortimer overthrew Edward II, forced him to surrender his crown, and had the young Edward crowned Edward III. Edward II was imprisoned and later brutally murdered. It was this act that gave Isabella the famous nickname bestowed on her by the poet Thomas Gray centuries later:

> The She Wolf of France, with unrelenting fangs
> That tearest the bowels of thy mangled mate.[3]

pass through the female line. For this reason the twelve peers and the barons of France gave the throne by common accord to the lord Charles of Valois . . . leaving out of the succession the Queen of England and her son who was the next male heir. . . . This is the point from which the afflictions and tribulations of war afterwards arose.[5]

The French had three other reasons for not wishing Isabella's son on their throne. First, he was only a boy of fifteen, whereas Philip was thirty-five and a famous warrior. Second, Edward was completely controlled by his mother and Mortimer. As Seward wrote, "[The French] had had the opportunity to see Isabella and her appalling lover . . . and had no

wish to be ruled by them."[6] Third, Edward was considered a foreigner; even though he was a duke of France, his heritage was French, and his native language was French.

After Philip of Valois became king of France, he ordered Edward III to appear before him to once again do homage for Guyenne. The fifteen-year-old Edward, still under the control of Isabella and Mortimer and weakened by quarrels within his own kingdom, had no choice. In June 1329 in a ceremony in Amiens, he placed his hands between those of Philip and was asked, "'Sir, will you become the liegeman [vassal] of the King of France, as duke of Guyenne and a peer of France, and will you promise to bear faith and loyalty to him?' Edward answered, 'Truly.'"[7]

A King's Revenge

When he was young, Edward III was under the control of his mother's lover, Roger de Mortimer, earl of March. The young king plotted to gain his freedom. When the end came for Mortimer, it was swift, according to Geoffrey le Baker's Chronicle, *quoted in Myers's* English Historical Documents:

"The constable led his lord the king by tortuous ascents through a certain secret subterranean tunnel. . . . Having rushed out of the underground passage and subterranean route, the king's friends advanced with drawn swords to the queen's bedroom; the king waited armed, outside the chamber of their foes, lest he should be seen by his mother. . . . Then they found the queen mother almost ready for bed, and the Earl of March, whom they wanted. They led him captive into the hall, while the queen cried, 'Fair son, fair son, have pity on gentle Mortimer'; for she suspected that her son was there. . . . When the parliament of the realm sat at Westminster [Mortimer] was drawn and hanged on the common gallows of thieves at the Elms. So by his death he ended the civil wars which he often stirred up throughout his life."

Edward III Assumes Control

Edward III was tired of being Isabella and Mortimer's puppet. He wanted to rule on his own. When he returned to England, he began to gather around him a group of loyal, bold, young noblemen. They struck on October 19, 1330. Entering Nottingham Castle through a secret passage, they killed two guards, burst into Isabella and Mortimer's bedchamber, and seized Mortimer. The next month Mortimer was hanged as a traitor. At Edward's order the body was left hanging two days and two nights. Isabella was treated more gently by her son but was nevertheless confined to various castles for the remainder of her life.

Some of Mortimer's followers rebelled against the young king, and it took him two years to restore peace in England. He then turned to Scotland. Edward's grandfather, Edward I, had defeated the Scots and forced them to recognize him as king. The Scots won everything back from Edward II, however, humiliating the English army at Bannockburn in 1314.

Revenge on the Scots

In 1332 Edward III saw a chance to get revenge and once more establish English rule over the Scots. The king of Scotland was the eight-year-old David II, whose eleven-year-old wife, Joan, was Edward's sister. Although Edward sought revenge, he was afraid of provoking Philip into renewing the alliance between France and Scotland. He secretly aided a small group of rebel Scots, who won a series of swift victories. Their leader, Edward Baliol, was crowned king and acknowledged Edward as his overlord. David and Joan went into hiding.

After the Scots rallied and chased Baliol across the border in December, Edward marched north at the head of his army and surrounded the key city of Berwick on the coast. When the Scots sent their main army

England's King Edward I defeats the Scots in battle and forces them to recognize him as their king.

The Well-Dressed Warrior

Warfare was the chief occupation of the nobility of the Middle Ages. This excerpt from a fifteenth-century manuscript described how a man should be most comfortably armed when fighting on foot. It is found in A. R. Myers's English Historical Documents:

"He shall have no shirt upon him but a doublet [close-fitting jacket] of fustian [a type of cotton] lined with satin cut full of holes. The doublet must be strongly sewn where the points must be set about the upper part of the arm and breast before and behind, and gussets [reinforcing inserts] of mail [metal mesh] must be sewn to the doublet at the bend of the arm and under the arm. The arming points must be made of fine twine such as men use to make strings for crossbows, and they must be tied small and pointed as points. Also they must be waxed with shoemakers' wax and they will neither stretch nor break. He shall have a pair of hose [leggings] of worsted cloth and a pair of short pads of thin blanket to put about his knees against the chafing of his leg harness; also a pair of shoes of thick leather, and they must be fastened with stout whip-cord, three knots upon a cord, and three cords must be sewn fast unto the heel of the shoe and fine cords in the middle of the sole of the same shoe, and there must be in between the cords of the heel and those of the middle of the shoe the space of three fingers."

A medieval warrior wields a crossbow.

to save the city, they were soundly defeated at Halidon Hill in July 1334. This battle was, militarily, a preview of some of the principal battles of the Hundred Years' War. Edward took up a defensive position on a hill. His men-at-arms (those with armor and horses) dismounted. Flanking them were rows of archers with longbows.

The Scots had faced longbows before. The Welsh, serving under Edward I, had used them so effectively that one Scottish commander decreed that every captured English archer should have his left hand cut off. In France the longbow was unknown. Instead, the crossbow was used. It was more accurate and had a longer range but was slow to use. After each shot the archer had to crank the bowstring into place. Five longbow shots could be fired in the time it took a crossbowman to reload.

But the Scots had not learned from previous defeats. They charged up the hill under a rain of arrows. The few who reached the top were easily cut down by the men-at-arms. Edward had his revenge. After the victory he burned villages and crops throughout a wide area and carried off everything of value. Both the tactics of the battle and the measures taken afterward were to be repeated on the plains of France.

The victory created Edward III's reputation as a commander. Jean le Bel took part in the campaign and later wrote a chronicle of the time. He wrote that when the king returned to England, he was

> universally loved and honored by high and low, as much for his noble words and deeds as for his greatness of heart and for the fair assemblies of ladies and maidens that he held, so much so that one and all said that he was King Arthur come again.[8]

A medieval army attacks a castle with crossbows and longbows before the men-at-arms storm it.

A Crusade Is Suggested

Meanwhile, all was peaceful between Edward and Philip of France. Their representatives met frequently to try to settle disputes about Guyenne. Edward had his hands full in Scotland and was in no position for war with France. Philip wanted to start a war, but not against England. In 1332 Pope John XXII suggested that Philip lead a great crusade against the Turks. Edward agreed to participate but said he would leave the "preparation and the glory of command" to Philip.[9]

Philip built a huge fleet at Marseilles on the southern coast of France. Sailing was set for May 1, 1336. Long before then, however, Philip's eyes were opened to what Edward had been up to in Scotland. Just as it appeared that a peaceful solution in Guyenne would be reached, David and Joan of Scotland sought refuge in France. Philip said that any agreement about Guyenne would have to include the restoration of David to the throne of Scotland. The Franco-Scottish alliance was renewed, and chances for peace disappeared. Historian May McKisack wrote, "From this time onwards, the support lent by Philip VI to Scotland remained as a major obstacle to the conclusion of an Anglo-French agreement and as a dangerous threat to the peace of western Europe."[10]

A new pope, Benedict XII, had tried to make peace between Edward and Philip. He obtained a short truce between England and Scotland in 1335 but made a serious error the next spring. Philip went to the pope, urging that the crusade go ahead as planned. Benedict, hoping to force a treaty, said that peace in Europe must come first. He canceled the crusade altogether.

Philip was furious. He thought the pope had tricked him by promising a crusade to prevent him from attacking Edward. He declared himself on the side of Scotland and transferred his fleet from the Mediterranean to the English Channel, poised to sail to Scotland—or England.

Robert of Artois

Edward now thought war was inevitable. Moreover, Robert of Artois, a French nobleman seeking revenge against Philip, was trying to convince Edward of his claim to the French throne. Robert had been found guilty of trying to use forged documents to take the lordship of Artois from his aunt. Later, when the aunt mysteriously died, Robert was accused of poisoning her. Philip had banished him from the kingdom and "let it be known that he would take up arms against anyone who gave him asylum."[11] Robert fled to England and was welcomed by King Edward III. According to Froissart:

He [Robert] was continually encouraging the King to defy the King of France, who was withholding his inheritance from him. And the King was in constant consultation with his privy council [advisers], deliberating how to maintain his right to the French throne of which he had been deprived in youth, but to which he was the rightful heir, as Count Robert of Artois had informed him.[12]

Edward began bargaining for formal military alliances in Flanders and in the cloth-producing county of Hainault and duchy of Brabant, which depended heavily on English wool. In 1336 Parliament (England's legislative assembly made up of the nobility and elected representatives) denounced the "perfidious [unscrupulous] maneuvers of the King of France."[13] It voted money for Edward to equip an army for war with France.

Philip took action. On May 24, 1337, he declared that Edward had forfeited Guyenne "because of the many excesses, rebellious and disobedient acts committed by the King of England against us and our Royal Majesty."[14] The declaration specifically mentioned Edward's protection of Robert of Artois.

Edward had gained allies by paying hard cash for them. He sent ambassadors, carrying plenty of gold, to the town of Valenciennes in Hainault. Before long, "a veritable market in alliances was flourishing" with nearby countries.[15] Finally, Edward felt strong enough to act. On October 7, 1337, he sent a letter of defiance to "Philip, who calls himself King of France," saying that he—Edward Plantagenet—was the rightful monarch."[16] The Hundred Years' War had begun.

2 France and England

When King Edward III of England challenged France, it must have seemed to the people of the time like the boy David challenging the giant Goliath. France was considered the most powerful nation in Europe. England was thought to be small, poor, and weak. The powerful country, however, had some weaknesses, and the weak country had some hidden strengths.

England's King Edward III challenged the king of France to battle for his throne. Many at that time thought powerful France would easily defeat England.

It would have been hard, indeed, for anyone to think that England would be a threat to France. Perroy wrote:

> An impartial observer trying to estimate the opposing forces in 1328 is immediately struck by the crushing disproportion—though it was doubtless more apparent than real—between the fame and wealth of the glorious kingdom of France and the weakness and poverty of the little kingdom of England. Among the two adversaries about to engage in a conflict of such unforeseen duration, no one could have predicted the reversal of strength which, to the great astonishment of contemporaries, put the heirs of Saint Louis [the French] in peril and raised those of the Plantagenets to the heights of power.[17]

The Might of France

France was large, though not as large as today. There were no exact borders beyond which the authority of a king stopped. The kings of France were so powerful that, in addition to the lands they ruled directly, they had great influence over local lords of neighboring lands, who were technically vassals of other kings.

France was also rich. Although trade and commerce were growing in Europe, most wealth still came from the land. In France the process of clearing forests and draining marshes to create land for crops and livestock was more advanced than anywhere else. More crops and livestock meant more wealth for those who raised them. This led to more towns and villages and to an increase in population. The population of France was about thirteen million, three times that of England. Froissart was impressed enough to write that "one may well marvel at the noble realm of France, therein are so many towns and castles, both in the distant marches and in the heart of the realm."[18]

France had flourished primarily because it maintained a strong central monarchy.

By armed conquest, inheritance, and marriage, the Capetian kings had greatly expanded the royal territory. Matthew Paris had written in the thirteenth century that "the King of France is the king of all earthly kings."[19] Within this territory, peaceful conditions prevailed and wealth grew.

The royal territory, however, did not extend to all of France. Large areas still were ruled by the great dukes. In Brittany, Burgundy, Flanders, and Guyenne (where the duke was also the king of England), the king of France had little control. This left him vulnerable to the shifting loyalties of his dukes.

Philip VI also was strengthened by his influence over the pope, head of the Catholic church. Philip the Fair had succeeded in moving the papacy to France in 1309. This meant that, for most of the

Blindfolds for Glory

Part of the code of chivalry, by which knights lived, was to do deeds of bravery in order to win the admiration of women. Jean Froissart describes in his Chronicles *how the English went to France in search of glory:*

"Then King Edward ordained ten bannerets [knights with their own banners] and forty other knights and sent them over the sea to Valenciennes, and the Bishop of Lincoln with them, to the intent to treat [negotiate] with the lords of the Empire, such as the Count of Hainault had named. When they were come to Valenciennes, each of them kept a great estate and port, and spared nothing, no more than if the King of England had been there in proper person, whereby they did get great renown and praise. They had with them young bachelors, who had each of them one of their eyes closed with a piece of silk: it was said how they had made a vow among the ladies of their country, that they would not see but with one eye, till they had done some deeds of arms in France."

The coronation of a new pope. The pope resided in France from 1309 to 1377, during which time he was a powerful ally to the king of France.

century, French-born popes, living in France, supported the French monarchy.

France was also considered militarily superior to England. The army of Philip VI was thought to be the finest in the world—"strong of limb and stout of heart, in great abundance,"[20] according to Froissart. Philip himself had a reputation as the finest soldier in Europe.

The heart of the French army was the nobility, for whom fighting was a way of life. Fowler wrote that "above all they [the nobles] were drawn together by the noble profession of arms, by a knight's ability to fight on horseback with lance, sword and heavy armour, and by the income necessary to sustain these things."[21] The common soldiers, who went on foot and wielded pikes or bows, were considered by the nobles to be relatively unimportant to the outcome of battles. As it happened, the common soldiers would be crucial, and it would be the French nobility that would suffer during the Hundred Years' War because of this "increasing spirit of caste."[22]

Yet Philip had military problems. Because of the feudal system, which required a vassal to fight for his overlord only a

French knights compete in a tournament. The French army had a great many highly trained, experienced knights who kept themselves battle ready with such tournaments.

limited number of days each year (usually forty), his army could not be depended on for a long campaign. Also, each vassal was supposed to make his entire force available to the king. Over time, however, it became customary for only part—sometimes only a tenth—of a vassal's army to be sent to fight.

The other method of raising an army was to buy one. Hiring professional soldiers was common. This made long-term preparations for war and long campaigns easier, but it was expensive. France had no system of taxes to provide its kings with the steady income necessary to hire soldiers for long periods of time. Instead, a special tax had to be collected when a military emergency arose. These taxes were unpopular and could be collected only after war had been declared.

The Isolation of England

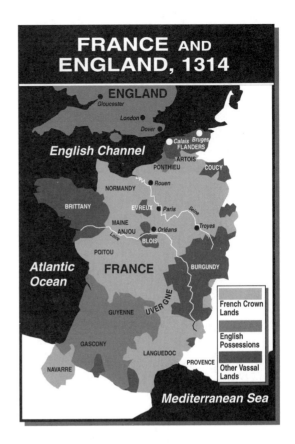

For most of the Middle Ages France had played a leading role in Europe. England, on the other hand, played almost no part at all. It was far away, geographically, from the center of affairs and, as an island, was especially isolated. It was considered poor and weak by the rest of Europe. The Plantagenets were more important as nobles of France than kings of England.

One reason for England's weakness was that the British Isles were far from united. Although Wales had been conquered by Edward I, Scotland remained a constant source of conflict. Ireland, except for a small area around Dublin called "the Pale," was unconquered and ruled by local chiefs.

England was nowhere near as wealthy as France. It was far smaller and much less populated. It was so much poorer that the income from the duchy of Guyenne in 1307 was greater than that of all England. Almost no manufacturing took place, as it did in France, and foreign trade was mostly done by foreigners who set up shop in London. Finance and banking were handled by representatives of the great banks of Italy.

England's land and climate were less suited to farming than France's, so less livestock and fewer crops were raised. Vast stretches of land were still covered with forests. Yet the plains of the southwest and the moors of the north were ideal for raising sheep. English wool was the finest in the world. The country would have been poor, indeed, without its wool trade.

Most wool was exported to the great cloth-making towns in Flanders.

The wool trade also enhanced England's military strength. The wealth of Flanders and surrounding countries depended on cloth making, and the cloth required wool. These countries and England were so economically linked that it was natural that Edward would look to these nations first when he needed military help against France.

Though the king of England's income was not as large as that of the king of France, it was more stable. He received a regular tax on all exported wool and large sums from seaports to give them exclusive rights to export wool. The English Parliament granted taxes frequently. These taxes were less unpopular than in France because they were voted by representatives of the people (the nobles and leading merchants, not the common people) instead of imposed by the king. Still, the royal incomes of both countries were too small to finance a large war, and both kings were forced to borrow huge amounts.

The English Nobility

As in France, the nobility made up the core of the English army. Yet the structure of the English nobility was far different. William the Conqueror saw firsthand the potential danger to the king from a too powerful vassal. Therefore, when he gave grants of land to his followers, the lands were in small-to-medium-size pieces throughout England. This prevented the earls of England from concentrating their power in a large area, as did the dukes and counts of France.

This limitation on the nobility should have made the king stronger. The English nobility, however, was unruly, and according to Fowler, "the ability of the king to govern effectively ultimately depended upon his relations with the magnates [nobles] of his realm."[23] Awareness of their power had come early to the English barons. A Frenchman in 1444 wrote, "They have a way in England of not thinking twice about changing their kings when it seems convenient, to kill them or evilly bring about their death—something the good and loyal people of France have never done."[24]

Constant wars, however, gave the king of England an advantage over the king of France in recruiting and keeping an army. Military service in England had come to be based on pay rather than on feudal duty: soldiers did not simply march home when their forty days were up. Another important difference was the way in which common soldiers were enlisted. In France they were either in the service of one of the king's vassals or were hired mercenaries. England, however, had commissions of array, much like a modern-day draft. As Fowler described it:

> Commissioners appointed by the Crown surveyed the able-bodied men in each hundred [a unit of land], township, and liberty [village] within the shire, selecting the best of them to serve at the king's wages. The commissioners themselves were normally men of the knightly class . . . who sought out men to make up their contingents. They were experienced staff officers who knew what they were looking for and may be presumed to have chosen well. Their efforts were assisted by

A Rich Man's Sport

When the upper classes were not fighting, they were hunting, an activity that was strictly reserved for the nobility. The parliamentary petition that follows, from 1390, prohibited the common people from participating in the sport. It is from English Historical Documents, *edited by A. R. Myers.*

"Also pray [ask] the Commons that whereas artificers [workers] and labourers, that is to say, butchers, shoemakers, tailors, and other low persons, keep greyhounds and other dogs, and at times when good Christians on holy days are at church, hearing divine services, go hunting in packs, rabbit-runs, and warrens of lords and others, and destroy them entirely; and so they assemble at such times to hold discussions, and make plots and conspiracies, to make insurrections and disobedience to your majesty and laws, under colour of such manner of hunting. May it please you to ordain in this present Parliament, that any kind of artificer or labourer or any other who lacks lands and tenements to the value of 40 [shillings] a year, or any priest or clerk if he has not preferment [income] worth [10 pounds], shall not keep any greyhounds, or any other dogs, if they are not fastened up or leashed, or have had their claws cut, on pain of imprisonment for a year. And that every justice of the peace shall have power to enquire and punish every contradiction."

proclamations issued at the beginning of each campaign, offering inducements to all and sundry to serve in the wars. Pardons for criminal offenses, the prospect of good wages and of a share in the incidental profits of war [loot and ransom] attracted many to active service. The troops so raised were technically conscripts [draftees] and compulsion may have had to be applied for service in Scotland; but there was no lack of volunteers for the campaigns in France, with their infinitely more attractive prospects of material reward.[25]

Edward III of England

In the Middle Ages the personality of individual kings was just as important as the size of each of their armies. The kings were expected to lead their armies personally and engage in hand-to-hand combat with their enemies. The valor of a king in battle and his skill as a general had much to do with the loyalty of his troops. This was part of the feudal idea of loyalty to an individual. Perhaps England's greatest asset in the first half of the Hundred Years' War was its king, Edward III.

A medieval manuscript illumination depicts a battle between the French and English.

Edward's personality is difficult to understand. His personality was typical of an age of great contradictions. He was said to have great charm. He often gave rich gifts and lavish hospitality to a conquered foe. On the other hand, he could order the slaughter of innocent men, women, and children in towns that stubbornly held out against him. At times he was "England's happiest king," heroic, chivalrous, brave, wise.[26] At other times he seemed no more than an ambitious adventurer willing to go to any lengths, however brutal or unethical. He borrowed money from everyone and anyone to finance his wars, without a thought about how he would repay. Often he did not, and those from whom he borrowed were ruined.

Physically, he was extremely tall, with long, blond hair and mustache and a pointed beard. Unlike his father he was respected for his fighting ability. In addition, the willingness of the English to fight in and pay for Edward's war is evidence of his ability to win "the loyalty of his people and affections of his magnates."[27]

Edward was clearly a superior general to Philip of France. In addition to relying on his archers, Edward successfully used a tactic that had been forgotten since the legions of Rome: coordinated attacks by separate forces that advanced from different directions. Perroy called Edward "an opportunist of genius, who used his adversary's difficulties to the full, and constantly modified the detail of his plans in order to adapt them to changing circumstances."[28]

Philip VI of France

Philip VI was widely respected as a fighter and was famous throughout Europe for his accomplishments on the battlefield and in tournaments. He was less successful as a ruler and as a general. He was overconfident of his own ability and refused to learn from experience. When his opponents changed tactics, he refused to change with them.

Even though Philip was brave, he was not an inspiring leader. While the English readily followed Edward across the water to France, the French nobility was slow to support Philip as he resisted the invasion of their own country. Michael Packe said that Philip was "a mediocrity" and that he "would never be able to stir his Frenchmen as the flamboyant Edward led his English."[29]

Philip's pride led him to seriously underestimate his opponent, Edward. This was not entirely his fault. He received bad advice from his counselors, who urged him to follow the same policy France had used against Edward II, who had easily been kept a meek vassal. "What the advisers of the King of France did not understand," wrote Perroy, "was that these easy times were gone, and that, with Edward III firmly seated on his throne, the French monarchy had found an adversary of its own weight."[30]

It was this adversary, Edward III, who started the Hundred Years' War. Why he started it remains something of a mystery. He may not have truly believed in his right to the throne of France but only tried to use the claim to secure his rule over Guyenne. Or, he simply may have been eager for a war. Fighting, whether in war or in tournaments, was a way of life for the nobility. As McKisack wrote, "the fact that the captains and the kings enjoyed it was

King Edward III of England possessed a charismatic personality and a superior military savvy that were England's greatest asset in the Hundred Years' War.

King Philip VI of France was a renowned warrior but proved to be only a mediocre ruler and general. Pride and overconfidence led to his undoing.

not the least important reason why the war was fought."[31] So, despite the claim to the throne, the conflict about authority over Guyenne, and the alliance of France with Scotland, the principal reason Edward went to war may well have been simply because he wanted to.

So even though, in 1337, England was smaller and weaker than France, the island nation had some hidden advantages. France, on the other hand, had some hidden weaknesses. Each would become apparent as the war progressed. "It is important to bear in mind," Perroy wrote, "that at the moment when a change of dynasty took place in France, England, which had barely emerged from civil war, was politically powerless, though, thanks to the resources which the monarchy had at its disposal, she was capable of rapid recovery."[32]

Chapter

3   Sluys, Crécy, and Calais

Although Edward III of England declared himself the rightful king of France in 1337, he was nowhere near ready to enforce his claim by force; he first needed allies.

For two years after Edward's declaration, little actual fighting took place, as he gathered allies. One was William of Hainault, his father-in-law.

Edward also bought alliances with Gelderland, Brabant, Juliers, and Limburg. These small countries, like Hainault,

were part of the Holy Roman Empire, a large area that included today's Germany, Austria, and the Netherlands. In exchange for a huge amount of money, the Holy Roman emperor himself, Ludwig IV, made Edward deputy of all the empire west of the Rhine River.

Flanders was different. Although the merchants of Flanders had strong economic ties to England because of the wool trade, the count of Flanders was a vassal of the king of France. Edward was able to

Ships from Ghent attack the castle of the count of Flanders. These neighbors were drawn into the fighting of the Hundred Years' War.

encourage the merchants, who were led by wealthy brewer Jacob van Artevelde, to revolt. The French count had to flee to Paris.

Edward Seeks Battle

By 1339 Edward had spent a fortune and had yet to fight a battle. He had borrowed everywhere and even pawned the great crown of England. He could wait no longer. In September 1339 he led a small English army and some allies into France from Flanders. Hoping to draw Philip into battle, he marched south, slaughtering livestock, burning crops and villages, and killing peasants.

Edward had learned this new form of total war in Scotland. Called a *chevauchée* ("a run through on horseback"), it was intended to make the common people sick of war and to weaken the local government. The English employed it again and again, bringing great misery to the people of France. The French, in turn, developed a hatred of the English that would last for centuries.

The French army marched north from Paris and confronted the English near Saint-Quentin. Edward sent a challenge to Philip, and the French king, much to Edward's joy, replied that "if [Edward] would choose out a place not fortified with trees, ditches or bogs, the King of France would without fail afford him battle."[33] But Philip changed his mind. With the armies in position, the French king hesitated and finally withdrew altogether, unwilling to take the risk of losing.

Edward was furious at the waste of time and money. He returned to Flanders,

Buying Friends for Cash

Although it was a time in which nobles were concerned about personal honor, military alliances were up for sale. James MacKinnon describes the practice in The History of Edward the Third:

"For these handsome gratuities [payments] they [Edward III's allies] undertook to place a certain number of men-at-arms at Edward's disposal in the forthcoming conflict, Ludwig's quota being two thousand men. In those days alliances were knocked down to the highest bidder, and, as alliance merely meant, in the meantime, promises which cost but words, the Bishop of Lincoln did a roaring business. Should Philip afterward come in and bid higher, there was nothing in the political morality of the time to prevent the Duke of Brabant from transferring his troth [loyalty]. If one royal bidder was fool enough to pay him to make war, why should not his antagonist pay him not to make it? Anything in the way of business was the political ethics of the age."

England's King Edward III sits enthroned (left) in garments emblazoned with the fleur-de-lis *of the French kings.*

where the merchants who had loaned him money grumbled about his lack of success. On February 6, 1340, he formally declared himself king of France, hoping that Flanders would obey him more readily if he were their king instead of only an ally. The royal coat of arms was redesigned to include the lilies (*fleur-de-lis*) of France alongside the lions of England. Although the Hundred Years' War ended in 1453, Edward's descendants would not formally renounce this claim to the French throne until 1802.

The Flemings (the people of Flanders) were impressed, but not completely so. They allowed Edward to return to England with his eldest son to raise more money but forced him to leave the pregnant Philippa behind with two of the younger children. Their child John was born that spring in the city of Ghent and was known afterwards as John of Gaunt (the English spelling of Ghent).

Edward, by claiming that France was about to invade England by crossing the channel between the nations, persuaded Parliament to vote a tax to continue the war. Both countries wanted control of the English Channel. If the English controlled the channel, it would be easier for them to invade France. If the French controlled it, an invasion by England was impossible. French ships, the same ships Philip had moved from the Mediterranean to the channel in 1336, had begun raiding the southern coast of England. Parliament wanted Edward to prevent France from crossing the channel.

The Battle of Sluys

Philip may not have intended to invade England, but he did mean to control the English Channel. He massed his ships at the port of Sluys on the mouth of the Zwin

Edward Claims France's Throne

In 1340, partially in order to impress his allies, Edward III formally assumed the title of king of France. His proclamation appeared in Robert of Avesbury's De Gestis mirabilibus regis Edward Tertii (Of the Marvelous Life of King Edward III) *and is found in* English Historical Documents, *edited by A. R. Myers:*

"Since the kingdom of France has by divine disposition devolved [come] upon us by the clearest right owing to the death of Charles of noted memory, the last king of France, brother germane [having the same parents] to our lady mother, and the lord Philip of Valois, son of the king's uncle and thus farther removed in blood from the said king, and holds that kingdom against God and justice, lest we should seem to neglect our right and the gift of heavenly grace or to be unwilling to conform the impulse of our will to the divine pleasure, we have recognised our right to the kingdom and have undertaken the burden of the rule of that kingdom, as we ought to do, resolving with unshakable purpose to act with good and devoted servants, to do justice to all men according to the just and laudable [praisable] customs of all men, to revive the good laws and customs which were in force in the time of Louis, our predecessor, and to cast out that usurper [Philip] when opportunity shall seem most propitious [favorable]. . . . Given at Ghent on the 8th of February, in the first year of our reign over France and the 14th of our rule over England."

River, which flowed into the channel at the northernmost tip of France. Edward had been busy during the first half of 1340 building a fleet of his own, which sailed on June 22. The next day the French fleet was sighted and Edward "saw such a number of masts in front of him that it looked like a wood [forest]."[34]

On the morning of June 24 the English sailed toward the French and then suddenly turned, as if running away. The French chased them but were so numerous that they ran into one another in the narrow mouth of the harbor. Edward turned once more and, with the wind at his back and the sun in the Frenchmen's eyes, he attacked.

The English tactics were to crash into the French, fasten onto the enemy ships with grappling hooks, and swarm aboard. Before this was done, however, the English archers opened fire, raining arrows onto the French ships and killing men by the hundreds. The archers proved to make the difference between victory and defeat. By the time the ships came together, the French had lost any advantage of numbers.

The battle was long and hard. There was no place for the overwhelmed French to run. Hundreds jumped or were thrown into the sea. Few could swim, and the armored men, of course, sank like stones. Before the French were totally defeated, Edward was wounded in the thigh by an arrow.

Sluys was the first important battle of the war. Although England did not yet have complete control of the channel, the threat of a French invasion had vanished. In addition, Sluys gave Edward additional proof of the power of the English longbow. "With hindsight," a historian wrote, "one can see that Sluys marked the passing of the initiative to the English—indeed, to the men of 1340, God had shown he was on their side."[35]

It was a magnificent victory for Edward and a terrible defeat for Philip. For days nobody dared tell him what had happened. Finally, his jester said, "What cowards these English are." "How so?" asked the king. "Because," answered the jester,

The naval battle at Sluys in the English Channel was the first important battle of the Hundred Years' War. It was a decisive English victory.

"they are afraid to jump into the sea, as our brave Normans and Frenchmen did."[36]

Edward tried to follow his victory at sea with one on land, but his hired allies began to quarrel with one another and to head home when they were not paid promptly. Philip advanced against Edward with a large army but once more refused to do battle. In late September Edward, out of money again, agreed to a truce. Once back in England he turned his attention to raising more money, while waiting for another opportunity to invade France. Edward, wrote Michael Packe, "never regarded the truce as anything but a pause for breath to be concluded as soon as possible."[37]

Civil War in Brittany

Edward's opportunity came in Brittany, the westernmost county in France, where two people claimed the title of count. King Philip supported his niece, Jeanne of Blois. John of Montfort, Jeanne's rival, fled to England, where he acknowledged Edward as king of France in exchange for Edward's support.

Edward arrived in Brittany with twelve thousand troops in the fall of 1342. He began a *chevauchée* and threatened to capture the major cities. Philip sent an army commanded by his eldest son John, duke of Normandy. Once more, no battle took place. Pope Benedict intervened and persuaded the two sides to sign a truce in 1343, leaving the title of count still unresolved.

Edward was soon ready to resume the war and now devised a strategy of attacks from three directions. One would be led from Guyenne by the king's cousin, Henry (later the duke of Lancaster). The second would come from Brittany, led by Sir John Dagworth. The third would be led by Edward himself.

The first two came in 1345 and caught the French by surprise. Philip again gave command of his army to his son, John of Normandy, who marched south to Guyenne. When John finally reached Henry, he was safe in the heavily fortified city of Aiguillon. John settled down to starve the city into surrender.

Edward Lands in Normandy

This situation was what Edward had been waiting for. With the main French army in the south, he would attack in the north. On July 5, 1346, he sailed from Portsmouth with a thousand ships and fifteen thousand men. With him was his son, Edward of Woodstock, now almost sixteen years old and recently made prince of Wales. They landed at The Hague on July 12. Froissart described the landing:

When the King of England . . . issued out of his ship, and the first foot that he sent on the ground, he fell so rudely that the blood brast [burst] out of his nose. The knights that were about him took him up and said, "Sir, for God's sake enter again into your ship and come not on land this day, for this is but an evil sign for us." Then the king answered quickly and said, "Wherefore [why]? This is a good to-

The English attack and lay waste to the French city of Caen.

King Edward III prays for victory before going into battle at Crécy.

ken for me, for the land desireth to have me." Of which answer all his men were right joyful.[38]

The Normans were surprised and unprepared. Edward began a *chevauchée,* "deliberately devastating the rich countryside, his men burning mills and barns, orchards, haystacks and cornricks, smashing wine vats, tearing down and setting fire to the thatched cabins of the villagers, whose throats they cut together with those of their livestock."[39] On July 26 the English stormed into Caen, killing more than three thousand civilians.

Philip now called together an army, not as large as his son's in Guyenne, but far larger than Edward's. Edward marched toward Rouen, the capital of Normandy, on the Seine River between Paris and the English Channel. Philip advanced quickly

and reached the city on August 2, before the English. His plan was good, but he made one fatal mistake. He determined to defeat Edward himself and did not call on his son John to come to his aid until it was too late.

Edward now had to choose a plan of his own. Philip had left Paris undefended, but Edward had to assume that John was on his way from the south. Edward moved toward Paris, hoping to lure Philip back to his capital. With Philip back in Paris, Edward would be free to head north to join with his Flemish allies, who had begun marching south on August 2. The English king's plan worked. When Edward reached a point only twenty miles from Paris, Philip raced ahead of him and reentered the city.

Edward rapidly headed north. Philip, now seeing what his enemy intended, gave chase. Edward moved quickly, but Philip moved even faster and, on August 21, reached the city of Amiens on the Somme River, blocking Edward's path. Edward headed northwest, toward the sea, hoping to find a place to cross the Somme River before Philip caught up with him. A peasant named Gobin Agache, seeking a reward, showed Edward a place where the river could be crossed at low tide. The English crossed over, and by the time Philip arrived the tide had come in and swollen the river so that his army was unable to cross.

The Battle of Crécy

Edward hoped the Flemings would be near, but they were nowhere to be found. His army was hungry and exhausted. Edward knew he would have to turn and face Philip alone. On August 25 he halted his troops near the village of Crécy. Crossing the river had given him time to choose a position on a hill with a forest at his back and a little river to his right. The only way for the French to attack was to come up the hill.

A Teenage Warrior

Although he was only sixteen years old, Edward of Woodstock, the Black Prince, proved his ability at the Battle of Crécy as described in Geoffrey le Baker's Chronicle *found in Meyers's* English Historical Documents:

"In such a woeful encounter Edward of Woodstock, the king's eldest son, being then sixteen years old, in the first division showed his valour to the French, piercing horses, laying low the riders, shattering helmets and breaking spears, skillfully parrying [deflecting] blows aimed against him, helping his men, defending himself, helping to their feet friends who had fallen, and showing to all an example in well-doing. He did not rest from his great labours until the foes, protected by the rampart [wall] of dead men, retreated. There his knightly honour learnt how he might skillfully perform knightly deeds at the battle of Poitiers, at which later he captured the King of France. . . . Then someone ran or rode to the king his father, and, pointing out the peril which beset his eldest son, implored help; so he was sent with twenty knights to help the prince and found him and his men leaning on spears and swords, taking breath and resting quietly on long mounds of corpses, waiting for the enemy who had withdrawn."

The Battle of Crécy changed the face of warfare by proving bowmen were superior to armored cavalry.

On the morning of August 26 Edward III "went among his men, exhorting each of them with a laugh to do his duty, and flattered and encouraged them to such an extent that cowards became brave men."[40] He divided his forces into three battles, or divisions. One was commanded by his son, Prince Edward. Many years afterward a story was told that the prince wore black armor of burnished steel at Crécy. From this he acquired the famous name of the Black Prince, though it was never used in his lifetime.

Philip hurried to catch Edward. His horses were tired, and many of his foot soldiers had not arrived. He wanted to wait until his army was fresh. His commanders, however, had been looking forward to such a battle for years; they wanted no more delays. Philip realized he had no choice and, in the late afternoon, ordered the attack to begin.

Philip's hired crossbowmen from Genoa in Italy were the first to advance, but before they could start, a sudden, brief thunderstorm struck. By the time they started up the hill, the ground was slippery and the sun was in their eyes. Just as the Genoese began to shoot, the English archers "let their arrows fly in such unison that they were as thick as snow."[41] The Genoese broke and ran back into the path of the French cavalry. "Kill this rabble, kill them!" shouted Philip. "They are getting in our way and they serve no purpose."[42] The French knights obeyed, riding down and killing many of the retreating Genoese. All the while, the deadly hail of English arrows continued.

The bearded King John of Bohemia lies slain on the blood-soaked battlefield at Crécy.

The French knights then charged. Those not killed by the English arrows were successful in reaching the top of the hill, only to be cut down by the axes and swords of the English men-at-arms, who had dismounted. The French charged sixteen times in all, and the battle lasted far into the night.

Finally, Philip, trying to mount a last charge, found he had only sixty mounted men left. He was persuaded to flee to a castle six miles away. When he arrived, he shouted to the lord of the castle, "Open your gate quickly, for this is the fortune [the future] of France."[43] Pausing only for a drink of water, he resumed his flight.

The English did not at first realize the extent of their victory. The next day they discovered that they had lost fewer than a hundred men. On the French side, more than ten thousand common soldiers lay dead, as well as more than fifteen hundred knights and nobles, including King John of Bohemia, the duke of Lorraine (Philip's nephew), the duke of Alençon (Philip's brother), and the count of Flanders.

The Battle of Crécy was one of the most important in the history of warfare. It was "a military revolution, the triumph of firepower [here meaning archery rather than guns] over armor."[44] It also gave Edward a reputation as the master soldier of Europe and earned the English respect as fighters that they had never enjoyed. For centuries the armored horseman had been the most effective weapon of war. Now he could be killed by a foot soldier shooting an armor-piercing arrow from hundreds of yards away. Even Froissart, who normally described only knightly deeds, wrote that "many people say that it was by their [the archers] shooting that the day was won."[45] Doubtless, the archers also realized the part they had played. Perhaps they saw that the wide gulf between noble and commoner was shrinking.

On to Calais

Edward was in no position to take advantage of his victory. His troops had been in France for six weeks and were tired. He had destroyed Philip's army, but Prince John's was on the way, having finally left Guyenne on August 20. But before ending the campaign, Edward had one more goal—to capture and keep a seaport to use as a permanent base from which to conquer France.

He chose Calais, at the very northern tip of France and only twelve miles across the English Channel from Dover, but the city was stronger than Edward expected. It could not be taken by force, and Edward settled down for a siege. The city's commander, Jean de Vienne, was determined to hold out until winter, when Edward would be forced to leave. Vienne reckoned without the "dogged and rather terrifying" stubbornness of the king of England.[46]

Rather than sail home when winter came, Edward built his own city of log huts outside the walls of Calais. Queen Philippa and her ladies came from England. Edward even established a market to which local farmers, eager for English gold, brought their goods, while the increasingly hungry people of Calais watched from their walls. In October he received good news from home. King David of Scotland had been captured, taken to London, and made a prisoner. David was captured when, hoping to take advantage of Edward's presence in France, he had invaded northern England. The northern barons united and slaughtered the Scots at Neville's Cross.

Calais was running out of food. Early in 1347 Vienne sent five hundred civilians out through the city gate so that he would not have to feed them. Edward refused to let them through the English lines, and they huddled outside the walls, many starving to death. In June Vienne sent a letter to Philip:

> Know, most dear and dread lord, that although the people are all well and in good spirits, the town has great need of corn, wine, and meal. Everything is eaten up—dogs, cats, horses—and we have nothing left to subsist on, unless we eat each other. You write me to hold out as long as there was anything to eat, and now we have reached the direst extremity. We have therefore agreed, if succour [help] come not immediately, to sally out into the open and fight for life or death. For we would rather die on the field with honor than eat each other. Wherefore, most dear and dread lord, make an effort to help us, for if remedy cannot be speedily devised you shall see no more letters from me, and the town will be lost and every soul within it.[47]

Calais city leaders offer their lives to King Edward in exchange for the lives of the citizens of Calais.

Philip finally appeared with an army to attempt to save Calais in late July. He camped on a hill overlooking the city and sent a challenge for Edward to fight. Edward, secure in his heavily fortified wooden town outside the city walls, refused. After three days Philip gave up and marched away, leaving Calais to its fate. The next day Jean de Vienne rode out to give up his sword and the keys to the city.

The Queen Begs for Mercy

Edward was determined to punish Calais for its stubborn resistance. He first announced that he would put everyone in the city to death. Then six city leaders came to the king with ropes around their necks, wearing only their shirts and offering themselves if Edward would spare the rest. Edward was prepared to execute them on the spot, but Philippa begged for mercy. Froissart wrote:

> The Queen of England, whose pregnancy was far advanced, then fell on her knees, and with tears in her eyes implored him, "Ah, my lord, since I have crossed the sea in great danger, I have never asked you any favor. But now I humbly beg you, for the Son of the Blessed Mary and for the love of me, to have mercy on these six men." The king looked at her for some minutes without speaking, and then said, "Ah, lady, I wish you were anywhere but here. You have entreated me in such a way that I cannot refuse. Therefore, though I do it with great reluctance, I hand them over to you.

Do as you like with them." The queen thanked him from the bottom of her heart, and had the halters removed from their necks. She took them to her rooms, had them clothed and gave them a good dinner. She then gave them six nobles each and had them escorted safely out of the camp.[48]

Edward was firm, however, that Calais would become English. He expelled all the citizens and gave their houses to his followers.

The fall of Calais was very important to the war. First, it gave Edward and the English kings who followed him a secure base of operations from which to attack France. Second, it freed England from having to depend on the ports of Flanders to import their goods. Now the all-important wool would enter through Calais.

Edward and Philippa returned to London in triumph on October 12. He had been away from his kingdom for fifteen months. His victories were celebrated with a series of tournaments and celebrations.

Philip, meanwhile, wanted revenge. He sought to invade England and called on the Estates to give him the necessary money. They refused and rebuked their king for his humiliating defeat at Crécy and the loss of Calais. A spokesman told him:

> You should know how . . . you went to these places [Crécy and Calais] honored and in great company, at great cost and at great expense, and how you were treated shamefully and sent back scurvily [contemptibly] and made to grant all manner of truces, even while the enemy were in your kingdom and upon it.[49]

Chapter

4 The Black Death, the Black Prince, and Poitiers

As England celebrated and France despaired, a greater disaster than war was about to strike. A terrible disease—the Black Death—had begun in central China in the mid-1340s and spread throughout the world. The plague reached France in January 1348. Fifty-six thousand people died in Marseilles within the month. At

No treatment or prayer helped this victim of the Black Death. The plague stopped the Hundred Years' War for about five years.

Avignon, home of the pope, sixty-two thousand died within three months.

In June the plague spread to England from a ship that had landed in the tiny port town of Melcombe. One of the sailors "had brought with him from Guyenne the seeds of the terrible pestilence."[50] As in France, the plague spread quickly. At Bristol it "raged to such a degree that the living were scarce able to bury the dead."[51]

The Black Death was bubonic plague, spread by infected rats and the fleas that lived on them. Experts estimate that between one-fourth and one-third of the population of Europe died from this disease during the years 1348–1350. The plague struck mostly in crowded towns and among the poor, where rats and fleas would be found. But the nobility was not immune. Edward III's daughter Joan died of the plague in Bordeaux. As an anonymous poet wrote:

> Sceptre and crown
> Must tumble down
> And in the dust be equal made
> With the poor crooked scythe and
> spade.[52]

Because of the plague, the Hundred Years' War came to almost a complete stop for about five years. Some skirmishing continued on the borders of Guyenne. A plot

THE BLACK DEATH, THE BLACK PRINCE, AND POITIERS ■ 41

A Sudden Lack of Labor

The devastation done by the Hundred Years' War was small compared to that done by the Black Death. For the first time in the history of Europe, there was a labor shortage, as recorded by Henry Knighton in his Chronicle *included in A. R. Myers's* English Historical Documents:

"After the pestilence many buildings both great and small in all cities, towns, and boroughs fell into total ruin for lack of inhabitants; similarly many small villages and hamlets became desolate and no houses were left in them, for all those who had dwelt in them were dead, and it seemed likely that many such little villages would never again be inhabited. In the following winter there was such a dearth [shortage] of servants for all kinds of work that, so men believed, there had scarcely ever been such a shortage before. For the beasts and cattle strayed in all direction without herdsmen, and all things were left without anyone to care for them. . . . Moreover all magnates of the realm, and lesser lords too, who had tenants, remitted the payment of the rents lest the tenants should go away, because of the scarcity of servants and the dearness [high price] of things—some half their rents, some more, some less, some for two years, some for three, some for one, according as they could come to arrangements with them. Similarly, those who had let [rented] lands by days' works [in exchange for a year's work] of a whole year, as is usual with bondsmen, had to waive and remit such works, and either pardon them entirely or accept them on easier terms, at a small rent, lest their houses should be irreparably ruined and the land remain uncultivated. And all victuals [food supplies] and all necessities became too dear."

to surrender Calais to the French was discovered late in 1349 and was put down by a small English force. In 1350 Edward led the English fleet to victory against ships from Castile in Spain.

This battle was the last victory and the last major battle for Edward III. Philip of Valois did not live to see it. The king of France had died two weeks before. Philip's throne passed to his son, John of Normandy. Edward, now almost forty, turned the leadership of the army over to his son Edward, the Black Prince.

Most of the fighting in the early 1350s was in Brittany, where Jeanne of Blois and John of Montfort still vied for the title of count. Although relatively unimportant to the outcome of the war, the fighting showed the two natures of war in the Middle Ages. Some people considered warfare almost a sport, others a deadly and serious way to make money.

The Battle of Thirty

The most famous example of war as "a magnificent but murderous kind of tourney [tournament]"[53] occurred at the so-called Battle of Thirty at the town of Ploërmel in 1351. The English commander of the town, which was attacked by the French, suggested that instead of a long siege a battle be fought between thirty knights chosen from each side.

Word of the battle spread, and people came from miles around to watch. The scene of the fight was decorated with banners and ribbons. Spectators, including sweethearts, cheered both sides as the knights "fought for the love of their ladies fair."[54] The long battle, fought on foot, finally ended when one of the Frenchmen cheated. He left the battlefield, mounted his horse, and charged the Englishmen, who were soon defeated. This unchivalrous ending did not prevent the story of the battle from being told and sung by minstrels all over Europe.

Warfare, however, was a business to a much greater extent than it was a game. It was a way for men—both nobles and commoners—to make fortunes. The two primary methods soldiers used were simply looting the countryside—grabbing and carrying off whatever they could—and holding prisoners for ransom. Ransom was the preferred method. "It was not the certainty of profit that lured men into the war," wrote Fowler, "but the chance, often

no more than one in a hundred, of hitting the jackpot."[55] Even a common foot soldier might earn a fortune if he were lucky enough to capture a nobleman. The nobleman's freedom then would be bought by his family, and the more important the prisoner, the higher the ransom.

The English who occupied parts of Brittany had little opportunity for either looting or ransom, so they hit upon a new way to make money. This was called the *pâtis*, or suffering. The English soldiers holding a town set an amount that every surrounding village had to pay. If a village did not pay, the soldiers would burn it and kill its people. The *pâtis* eventually spread to all parts of France that were held by the English. It helped fuel hatred of the English.

Not only soldiers grew rich. Some English back in England also enjoyed the spoils of war. Soldiers returned with goods that they gave to their families or sold. The chronicler Thomas Walsingham wrote that in 1348,

> There were few women who did not possess something from Caen, Calais or another town over the seas, such as clothing, furs and cushions. Table cloths and linen were seen in everybody's houses. Married women were decked in the trimmings of French matrons, and if the latter bemoaned their loss, the former exulted at their gain.[56]

Charles the Bad

No wonder the English wanted the war to resume. So did Edward, and he found a new ally. King Charles of Navarre (called Charles the Bad by his subjects) was a grandson of King Louis X of France.

Besides his tiny kingdom of Navarre, Charles was lord of large areas in Normandy and central France near Paris. As a grandson of Louis X, Charles would have had a better claim to the French throne than would Philip of Valois. However, he had been born in 1332, four years after the throne went to Philip.

Charles felt cheated. In 1351 he began plotting with Edward, telling the English king they could divide France between them. His real plan, however, was to turn his loyalty back toward France in exchange for new lands. He became a close friend of John's eldest son, fourteen-year-old Charles, and was rumored to be plotting with Charles to overthrow John. (Young Charles was known as the dauphin, having

Charles of Navarre, also called Charles the Bad, felt cheated out of the throne of France.

been given the county of Dauphiné by his grandfather, Philip. From then on, the heirs to the throne of France would be known by that name.)

The French, afraid of an alliance between Charles of Navarre and Edward, tried to negotiate a permanent peace treaty with England. In 1354 John agreed to a settlement that would have given almost half of France to Edward. But John came to his senses, backed out of the deal, and instead seized all of Charles's lands in Normandy.

This action gave Edward III the excuse he needed to renew the war. In 1355 Edward the Black Prince, who had been named duke of Guyenne by his father, led a brutal *chevauchée* that extended across southern France to the Mediterranean and back again—about six hundred miles. France was so shaken that the Estates voted enough taxes to allow John to assemble a large army to attack Edward.

Edward III responded in July 1356 with another two-way attack. Henry, duke of Lancaster, led an army from Normandy to join the Black Prince, who moved north from Guyenne. King John spoiled the plan by ordering all bridges over the Loire River destroyed so that Henry was unable to go south. Meanwhile, John led his army west, forcing Henry to retreat, then marched toward the Black Prince, who had been plundering his way northward.

The Battle of Poitiers

The prince reached the Loire in early September and, like Henry, was unable to cross. Then he learned that John was marching against him. He had no choice but to head back south. His small force was loaded with loot, and its pace was slow. John

The Prince Granted a Favor

As the years after Crécy passed, the Black Prince grew restless and wanted to return to France. A visit from the captal of Buch provided him the chance, as told in The Life of the Black Prince *by the herald of Sir John Chandos (a herald was an official whose duties were to announce proclamations and take oral messages between nobles or armies):*

"And at that time there came from Gascony [Guyenne] the doughty and valiant Captal, who was right brave and courageous and greatly beloved of everybody. He was welcomed right nobly. The Prince, who rejoiced greatly at his coming, took fresh courage. One day he said to the King his father and to the Queen his mother: 'Sire,' quoth he, 'for God's sake, you know well that thus it is, that in Gascony the noble and valiant knights cherish you so greatly that they suffer great pain for your war and to gain you honour, and yet they have no leader of your blood. Therefore if you were so advised as to send one of your sons they would be the bolder.' And every one said that he spoke truly. Then the King let summon his great parliament. All were of accord likewise to send the Prince into Gascony, because he was of such renown, and ordained forthwith that with him should go [many nobles]. When the matter was settled and the ordinance wholly performed, they sent to Plymouth to assemble all their ships, men-at-arms, and archers also, and their provisions: very rich was their array. After the term of two months he took leave of the King his father, of the Queen his mother and of all his brothers and sisters. Right sore grieved were they at heart when it came to his departing, for there you might see lady and damsel weep and make moan in complaints; the one wept for her husband, the other lamented for her lover."

moved much faster, catching the Black Prince near the city of Poitiers. The prince had never intended to fight a major battle. Now he and John faced one another, just as their fathers had ten years before.

The Black Prince was the most famous warrior in Europe. He "towered, spiritually by head and shoulders, over the outstanding men of his time, even above his remarkable father, Edward III,"[57] biographer John Harvey wrote. But, unlike Edward, the Black Prince lived only for war. He lacked his father's political skill and "could never be a calculating machine."[58]

John also loved fighting, but he had little skill as a military leader. Seward called him "probably the most stupid of all

French kings" and "pigheaded."[59] Frenchman Perroy was more kind, writing:

> He was known to be dashing and dar-
> ing and deeply imbued with the ideal
> of chivalry. . . . John was quick to take
> offense, and subject to terrible rages
> which were provoked by the vaguest
> suspicions. He struck without rhyme
> or reason at those whom he distrusted,
> and was incapable of letting these
> irrational hatreds subside. . . . The mis-
> fortune was that, at a tragic moment in
> its history, the crown of France was
> worn, not by an incapable man—the
> epithet would be too strong—but by a
> mediocrity. John was conscious, to be
> sure, of the dangers he ran, but he
> lacked sufficient strength of mind to
> face them.[60]

John had about thirty thousand men
to the prince's six thousand at Poitiers. His
advisers urged him to surround the English and starve them into surrender, but
John wanted a battle. On September 18 he
prepared to attack, but representatives of
the pope appeared and tried to negotiate
a truce. John demanded the surrender of
the Black Prince himself, plus a hundred
of his best knights. The prince refused.

The delay, however, gave the Black
Prince a chance to strengthen his position.
Actually, his lack of numbers turned out to
be his strength. All he could do was repeat
his father's strategy at Crécy and choose a
strong defensive position. The English
formed a line on a hill behind a hedge.
Archers were stationed on each side and
slightly in front of the main army, so that
arrows would come at the enemy from
both sides as well as the front.

The next morning the French king
sent three hundred horsemen against the

*An early portrait of England's Prince Edward,
the Black Prince. Edward was known as the best
warrior in Europe, but he did not have the
political skills of his father.*

hedge. They wore breastplates of armor to
protect themselves from arrows, but the
English archers, from each side, were able
to shoot into the unprotected flanks of the
horses. Many of the horses threw their riders. A few men reached the hedge but
were beaten back.

The main body of the French army remained. The first division to charge was
led by Charles, the dauphin. It advanced
on foot, a terrible error. The French had
missed the entire lesson of Crécy. The
battle had not been won by fighting on
foot, but, instead, by the combination of
archers and men-at-arms. The French
knights at Poitiers had no archers covering
their charge and also wore themselves out
marching in heavy armor.

Still, they reached the hedge, and the fighting became so fierce that the Black Prince, who was behind the front line with reserve troops, had to bring them up to help. At last the French retreated. The English got ready for the next attack. Geoffrey le Baker wrote, "In the meantime, some of our men laid their wounded under bushes and hedges out of the way; others, having worn out their own weapons, took the spears and swords from those whom they had overcome, and the archers hastened to extract arrows from the wretches who were only half dead." [61]

The battle done, a woman mourns the loss of a loved one found amidst the heaps of corpses.

The Final Charge

The second French division, led by the duke of Orléans, perhaps saw the fate of the first two charges, lost heart, and retreated. The last division, led by John himself, had been out of sight behind a ridge.

Medieval battles like that at Poitiers were fought at terrifyingly close quarters. The dead and wounded were often trampled by those still fighting.

When the six thousand fresh troops came into view, some of the English thought the battle was lost. A knight standing near the Black Prince said so, and the prince turned in fury saying, "You lie, you miserable coward, for while I am alive it is blasphemy to say we are conquered." [62]

John attacked. His men-at-arms were packed together closely, holding shields over their heads to deflect arrows. They reached the hedge and began to cut down the tired Englishmen. The Black Prince, roaring, charged with his last four hundred men, "teaching the enemy how furious warlike desperation could be." [63] The battle could have gone either way. Just then one of the Black Prince's captains, the captal (lord) of Buch, who had circled behind the French with sixty men-at-arms and a hundred archers, attacked from the rear.

The French panicked, wavered, and were broken. "The banners began to totter, the standard bearers fell down," wrote Geoffrey le Baker. "Dying men fell on others' blood, those who had fallen cried out and yielded up their spirits and deserted their listless bodies with fearful groans." [64]

King John of France surrenders at the Battle of Poitiers as the English soldiers contend for the honor of making his capture.

King John fought on with his younger son Philip at his side but was finally surrounded. A battle nearly broke out among the soldiers over who would get credit for his capture. To save himself, John said, "Gentlemen, take me quietly to my cousin, the prince. Do not quarrel about my capture, for I am such a great knight that I can make you all rich."[65] That evening the Black Prince himself, on his knees, served dinner to John. John probably had little appetite. For the first time in more than a hundred years, a king of France had been taken prisoner.

The Battle of Poitiers was relatively unimportant from the point of view of military history. It was a repeat of Crécy and showed how stubbornly the French clung to the old ways of battle. Its effect on the war and on the rest of the century, however, was enormous. Harvey called it "in some senses the turning point of the Middle Ages so far as England was concerned. . . . The principles upon which it was fought were to underlie the creation

and maintenance of the British Empire over the next six hundred years."[66]

The *Routiers*

The capture of the king and many leading nobles brought misery to France. Throughout the kingdom taxes were imposed and crops and livestock taken to raise money for ransoms. With the king gone and the dauphin only eighteen years old, the central government collapsed. Many soldiers—French, English, Guyennois, and German and Italian mercenaries—now banded together into so-called Free Companies or *routiers* (highwaymen) and terrorized the country, particularly in northern France. Although the *routiers* came from many nations, all were called English by the French, an indication of how hatred was forming between the two countries.

The *routiers* would organize under a captain, capture a castle, kill the inhabitants, and use it as a base from which to plunder the area. They "wasted [destroyed] all the country without cause, and robbed without sparing all that ever they could get, and violated and defiled women, old and young, without pity, and slew men, women, and children without mercy."[67] When they had taken everything worth taking, they moved on. A French writer of the time described what was left:

> The loss by fire of the village where I was born . . . is to be lamented, together with that of many others nearby. The vines in this region were not pruned or kept from rotting by the labors of men's hands. The fields were not sown or plowed. There were no cattle in the fields. No lambs or calves

bleated after their mothers in this region. No wayfarers went along the roads, carrying their best cheese and dairy produce to market. . . . Houses and churches no longer presented a smiling appearance with newly repaired roofs, but rather the lamentable spectacle of scattered smoking ruins to which they had been reduced by devouring flames. The pleasant sound of bells was heard, indeed, not as a summons to divine worship, but as a warning of hostile intentions, in order that men might seek out hiding places while the enemy were yet on the way. What more can I say?[68]

Revolt and the Jacquerie

The government was in chaos. With the king in captivity the Estates demanded that the dauphin be governed by a council. Charles the Bad hoped to be made king himself. He plotted with the bourgeoisie, or middle class, led by a cloth dealer named Etienne Marcel, who encouraged the citizens of Paris to riot against the dauphin. When the rioters got out of control, however, and attacked members of the bourgeoisie, Charles the Bad left the city. In February 1358 a mob broke into the dauphin's chamber and murdered two of his friends. He and his family fled the city.

In May the peasants in the countryside, driven to desperation by taxes and the *routiers,* rebelled. The revolt was called the Jacquerie because of the nickname Jacques Bonhomme (John Goodfellow) used to describe the average Frenchman. The Jacques, as the rebels were called, were even more brutal than the *routiers.* Froissart described how they "captured a knight and, having fastened him to a spit, roasted him before the eyes of his wife and forced her to eat some of her husband's flesh and then knocked her brains out."[69] The Jacques had no plan, only a thirst for revenge. Perroy wrote that they "were destructive, but with no aim and no tomorrow."[70]

Frenchmen were horrified. Charles the Bad was clever enough to gain popularity by leading a force that crushed the rebellion. Charles's former ally Marcel, however, had sided with the Jacques. He lost his support in Paris and was killed by his own former followers. The dauphin, meanwhile, had waited patiently. After Marcel's death he returned to Paris, cheered by the people who had chased him out six months earlier.

Charles the Bad now again approached Edward III, suggesting they divide France between them. The French had been negotiating with the English for the return of King John. The first agreement, in 1358, would set John's ransom at four

Rebel leader Etienne Marcel is beheaded in Paris by his former followers in the Jacquerie. His death made safe the dauphin's return to Paris.

million gold crowns and give Edward about a third of France. The dauphin agreed, but Edward wanted even more. He took back the first treaty and proposed a second, in March 1359, that would give him the entire western half of France. The French refused, and Edward used the refusal as an excuse to join forces with Charles the Bad in an attack against the French.

Edward led an army of about six thousand men. One of them was a poor man-at-arms named Geoffrey Chaucer, later to win fame as the first great English writer. The army landed at Calais on October 28. Edward's goal was a *chevauchée* that would end with his coronation as king of France at Reims. This result was not what Charles the Bad had intended, and he made peace with the dauphin.

Edward, now on his own, attacked Reims in December but found it too strong. He crossed eastward to Burgundy, was bought off by the duke there, and turned west toward Paris. Edward did not have enough men to attack Paris but hoped that the dauphin would come out and fight him. The dauphin wisely refused, and Edward marched south to Chartres. On April 13 his army was hit by a fierce hailstorm that killed many men and horses. Edward saw it as a sign from God. He also heeded the advice of his cousin, the duke of Lancaster, who told him, "My lord, we could lose more in one day than we have gained in twenty years." [71]

The Treaty of Brétigny

A new treaty was drawn up at the village of Brétigny on May 1, 1360. It was almost the same as the first treaty in 1358. John's ransom would be cut from four million to three million crowns, and there would be renunciations or concessions on each side. The renunciations provided that John would give Guyenne and many other areas to Edward in full sovereignty, rather than with Edward as vassal to John. In return, Edward would abandon his claim to the French throne.

The Treaty of Brétigny was signed in October 1360 at Calais, but there was an important difference from what had been agreed upon a few weeks before. The renunciations, though signed and sealed, were not exchanged. That ceremony was scheduled for the next year. "In appearance, this modification was small," Perroy wrote. "In fact, it was to have incalculable consequences." [72]

King John was allowed to return to France on July 8, 1360. Several hostages, including the king's brother and two younger sons, were to remain in England until John's full ransom was paid. When this was delayed, the royal relatives negotiated their own treaty in 1363, promising a large cash payment, the surrender of more territory, and the quick exchange of the renunciations. Edward allowed them to leave but insisted that the Estates agree to the treaty. When the Estates met, "the Dauphin and his councilors defended the crown's real interests [the interests of France] better than the king [John]. They were the heart and soul of resistance to the treaty and secured its rejection." [73]

An honorable man, John felt his word had been broken. He returned to England early in 1364, giving himself up as a prisoner. His spirit was broken. He became ill and died on April 8 at the age of forty-five. The dauphin, now King Charles V, was determined to undo the Treaty of Brétigny in any way he could. The chance for a lasting peace was gone. The Hundred Years' War would continue.

5 Charles the Wise

During the reign of Charles V of France England would lose almost all it had gained during the first twenty years of the Hundred Years' War. Charles did not win it back as the English had taken it—through great victories. Instead, he regained his kingdom by diplomacy and by small-scale fighting, nibbling here and there at the English.

That Charles V was nothing like his father or grandfather probably saved France.

Philip and John had been warriors. Charles was "of frail constitution, with a slender, sickly body, very different from those athletic giants."[74] He was a scholar and was known by his people as Charles the Wise.

He was the first king of France who did not personally lead his armies. He decided on policy but left command in the field to professionals. Most importantly, he saw that diplomacy was the only way to regain

Charles V and his wife are crowned as king and queen of France. Called by his people Charles the Wise, he was a scholar rather than a warrior.

France Finds a General

For the first twenty years of the Hundred Years' War, the French lacked any general who could compete with Edward III or his son. They finally found one in Bertrand du Guesclin, as described by James MacKinnon in The History of Edward the Third:

"Happily for France, fortune provided him [Charles V] with a fitting counterpart in the victor of Cocherel, the Breton [from Brittany] captain, whose military capacity Charles had the insight to discover and the good sense to use. This Bertrand [du Guesclin], born at the castle of La Motte de Bron in 1326, was a very devil of a boy, impertinent, ugly to a degree . . . , quarrelsome, ever fighting the boys of the district, and inciting them to strife, detested by his father and mother, who would have been right glad had chance drowned him in some pond; a lad of mettle [courage] at all events, just the promise of a character which that fighting age might develop into a fighting genius. He obtained his training in arms in the rough school of that Breton warfare, amid which he grew to manhood. In that struggle, he took the side of Charles of Blois, and his name became famous as early as the siege of Rennes in 1356. Eight years later, the capture of Mantes and Meuland, and the victory of Cocherel, for which Charles created him Count de Longueville, showed that France at last possessed a general. The combination of philosopher king and the consummate [complete] man of action is the turning point of the drama."

what had been lost. An English spy was correct when he reported in 1364:

> The policy of the new king is to give fair replies in words to the English until such time as he has recovered the hostages who are in England, or at least the most important; and meanwhile he will make war on the King of Navarre [Charles the Bad] and continue that of Brittany; and, under cover of the said wars, he will go on assembling men-at-arms; and, as soon as he has recovered the said hostages, he will make war in all parts on the English and on the principality [Guyenne] and he will recover what he has lost from the English and finally will destroy them.[75]

Charles V's Four Problems

Before Charles could think of fighting the English, however, he had to overcome some major problems. The first was

Charles the Bad, still plotting to take the throne. The second was the ongoing civil war in Brittany. The third was the allegiance of Flanders. The fourth was the problem of the *routiers,* who still scoured large parts of the countryside.

Charles addressed the problem of Charles the Bad first. Just after Charles V was crowned, he granted the title of duke of Burgundy to his younger brother Philip. Charles the Bad thought he had a better claim to that title and began a rebellion. But Charles the Bad's forces were defeated by those of the king under his new commander, Bertrand du Guesclin, soon to become France's foremost soldier. Charles the Bad would continue to make trouble but was never again a serious threat.

The civil war in Brittany finally ended when John of Montfort, backed by Edward III of England, defeated and killed Jeanne of Blois's husband, Charles, at the Battle of Auray in 1364. Although the English candidate for the title of count of Brittany had won, the terms of the Treaty of Brétigny called for Brittany to remain

French. Edward, therefore, allowed John of Montfort to do homage for Brittany to Charles V and removed his soldiers. This response kept Brittany under French rule and rid the area of English troops.

Charles V's third problem was whether Flanders would be an ally of England or of France. The heir of the present duke, Louis de Male, was a daughter, Margaret. Edward III wanted Margaret as a bride for his fifth son, Edmund. Louis favored this marriage, which would have made Edmund duke of Flanders and, naturally, an ally of England.

Charles wanted Margaret to marry his brother Philip, duke of Burgundy. Charles got his way by convincing the French pope, Urban V, to forbid the marriage of Margaret and Edmund. The pope raised no objection, however, to the marriage of Margaret and Philip.

This marriage meant that Flanders would remain French. At the time it seemed the wisest thing to do from Charles V's standpoint. It prevented Flanders from coming completely under

Philip and Margaret, the duke and duchess of Burgundy. Their marriage sealed the alliance between France and Flanders.

English control and becoming in northern France what Guyenne was in the south.

Much later, however, the Valois kings, as Seward wrote, "were to regret bitterly the union of these two vast fiefs."[76] Burgundy and Flanders were both rich and powerful. United, they were so powerful that their duke would be almost equal in power to the king of France.

The War in Spain

The problem of the *routiers* was solved, not in France, but in Spain. King Pedro the Cruel of Castile (a kingdom in northern Spain) was facing a revolt led by his half brother, Henry of Trastámara. When Henry asked the French for help, Charles V saw a chance to get the *routiers* out of France. In 1365 he provided money to Guesclin, who offered the *routiers* more than they could make by terrorizing the countryside to follow him to Spain to fight for Henry of Trastámara.

The little war in Spain was important to the Hundred Years' War because Pedro, forced out of Castile, sought help from the Black Prince in Guyenne, promising him a rich reward. The prince had not had a good war for ten years and was eager for glory. He marched into Castile and defeated Henry at the Battle of Nájera

A Trick to Gain Freedom

Bertrand du Guesclin, taken prisoner during the Black Prince's Spanish campaign, used the prince's high opinion of his own military reputation to win his freedom. Jean Froissart relates how in his Chronicles.

"Among the many prisoners taken in the late expedition was Sir Bertrand DuGuesclin; now it happened (as I have been informed) that one day while the prince was at Bordeaux, he called Sir Bertrand to him and asked how he was. 'My lord,' he replied, 'I never was better. Indeed I cannot be otherwise than well, for I am, though in prison, the most honoured knight in the world.' 'How so?' rejoined the prince. 'Why they say in France,' answered Sir Bertrand, 'that you are so much afraid of me, that you dare not set me free, and for this reason I think myself so much valued and honoured.' 'What! Sir Bertrand,' said the prince, 'do you imagine that we keep you a prisoner for fear of your prowess? By St. George it is not so; for, my good sir, if you will pay one hundred thousand francs you shall be free at once.' Sir Bertrand was anxious for liberty, and by this scheme obtained it; for in less than a month, the money was provided by the King of France and the Duke of Anjou."

King Pedro of Castile (center) promised the Black Prince a rich reward for military help, but later went back on the promise.

in 1367. Henry fled and Guesclin was made a prisoner.

Pedro was unable or unwilling, however, to pay the Black Prince his reward. The prince, in turn, was unable to pay his soldiers and had to impose high taxes throughout Guyenne and his other lands. These taxes were unpopular, not only in the prince's new territory, but also in Guyenne.

Guyenne had been loyal to England for centuries, but this was changing. The nobles of Guyenne were growing uncomfortable under the close, and costly, rule of the Black Prince. As Harvey wrote:

The Black Prince kept his court with a magnificence that threw the majority of the kings of Europe into the shade. Every day at his table were more than 80 knights and 320 esquires. Jousts and revels were held at Bordeaux and Angoulême on the pattern of those at London and Windsor. When the King of Cyprus, Peter de Lusignan, came to

Europe . . . he visited the courts of France, England, Burgundy, and Flanders, but declared that he "had done little until he had seen [the court of] the Prince of Wales."[77]

Appeals to the King of France

Two counts in Guyenne refused to allow the new taxes to be collected in their lands. When the prince insisted, they appealed to Edward III but, fearing what his answer would be, also appealed to Charles V. Charles was in a difficult position. According to the Treaty of Brétigny, Edward was sole ruler of Guyenne, but the renunciations had never been formally exchanged. In June 1368 Charles accepted the appeals but wanted them kept secret until he was strong enough to act.

Charles had been quietly building and reforming the French army. The taxes

Charles the Wise

King Charles V of France was completely unlike those who had ruled before him. James MacKinnon, in his History of Edward the Third, *gives this description of the man known as Charles the Wise:*

"When France was in danger of being submerged in the abyss of misery and anarchy, this king found time to collect some coveted literary treasure of classic antiquity or medieval lore for the library in the Louvre, or examine the plan of some new castle or church, or search out and reward some deserving scholar. Nor is it less novel in a century of crass injustice to find a monarch who would arrest the march of his army to hear the plaint [plea] of a poor widow who entreated his intervention in her cause, or ordered one of his suite [staff], found guilty of violating the daughter of his hostess, to be hanged on the nearest tree, or protected the Jews from the malice and the extortions of Christians. . . . A sovereign who was at once moralist, philosopher, theologian, scientist, as well as a conscientious and laborious administrator—and that sovereign a Valois—is indeed a phenomenon. Unlike his father and grandfather, he had no love of [military] camps, no predilection [desire] for knightly distinction. A malady with which he was attacked in his early days permanently shattered his health, and deprived him of the use of his right hand. He therefore left to rougher natures the uncongenial task of campaigning. For him the kingship was a charge [duty], not a dignity, and its main function consists in the power of doing good to others. . . . 'There never was a king who had less to do with arms,' said Edward [III], 'yet never was there a king who gave me so much to do.'"

imposed to collect King John's ransom were continued, even though no money was sent to England after John's death. The money was used to recruit troops and pay them on a regular basis. More importantly, Charles had learned from Crécy and Poitiers. "Interest was taken in the role, hitherto despised, which the infantry could play in combat," wrote Perroy.[78] As in England, men were commanded to practice archery.

Charles secretly accepted more appeals from nobles in Guyenne against the Black Prince. In January 1369 he announced that he was entitled to receive these appeals. He demanded that the prince come to Paris to answer the charges against him. The prince was furious, telling Charles's messengers, "We will willingly attend on the appointed day in Paris, since the King of France commands it, but it will be with our helmet on our head and sixty thousand men behind us." [79]

Edward III, at age fifty-six, was too old to fight. He unsuccessfully tried to get his son to abandon the high taxes. He tried to negotiate a peace with Charles, but the king of France was set on war. In June Charles, to show his contempt for the English, sent what Froissart called a "kitchen servant" to deliver a letter of defiance to Edward.[80] In the letter Charles declared that the English had forfeited Guyenne.

The War Resumes

When the war resumed it became clear that the French had learned new tactics but that the English had not. Guesclin, who had been ransomed and made constable (supreme commander) of France, defeated English strongholds in the north. The duke of Anjou attacked Guyenne in the south. Edward replied by using the tactics of the 1340s, the *chevauchée*.

Charles would not be lured into a major battle. Instead, the French relied on hit-and-run tactics. They encouraged local lords to declare their loyalty to Charles and promised them help if they did. One who did, and who regretted it, was the bishop of Limoges in Guyenne. The Black Prince besieged the city. When it fell, the prince took his revenge. "It was a great pity to see the men, women, and children kneel down on their knees before the

An effigy of Edward the Black Prince, who died an invalid in 1376. His father, Edward III, outlived him, so he never became king of England.

prince for mercy, but he was so inflamed with ire [anger] that he took no heed to them," wrote Froissart.[81] More than three thousand were massacred.

This was the end of the war for the Black Prince. In Spain he had caught a disease, probably dysentery, which had grown slowly worse. At Limoges he was barely able to mount a horse. In October 1372 he resigned as duke of Guyenne, returned to England, and became an invalid.

By 1374 almost everything the English had gained in thirty-seven years had been

Charles VI of France (center) was a boy of twelve when he took the throne.

lost. Calais remained, but the part of Guyenne controlled by the English was smaller than when war had been declared in 1337. It appeared that the English would be driven completely out of France, but both sides were now weary. Charles V was in poor health. French troops and the French treasury were exhausted. The Black Prince was slowly dying. Edward III had become an alcoholic, and John of Gaunt was the real power in England.

A New King in England

In 1377 England had a new king. The Black Prince had died in June 1376. Edward III died a year later. The crown went to the Black Prince's ten-year-old son Richard, who became King Richard II. His uncle, John of Gaunt, continued the war.

English raids in France continued but had little effect. In July 1380 Guesclin fell ill during a siege and died, and "there was no one to put new heart in the troops."[82] Just three months later his master, Charles V, died at the age of forty-three. His last official act, however, was to prove important. On his deathbed, concerned that he had overburdened his people, Charles abolished some of the high taxes, and "with the stroke of a pen he deprived his successor of the means [the income from the taxes] of governing."[83]

This phase of the war did not end with a treaty or a truce. Instead, it "began to peter out for want of coherent direction on either side."[84] Charles was succeeded by his son, Charles VI, a boy of twelve. Both England and France now had boy kings. Both kingdoms became divided as royal uncles sought to control their nephews. The war between the countries ground to a halt that would last thirty-five years. Perroy wrote, "By fits and starts, the two countries had outrun their strength."[85]

6 A Lengthy Interlude

The reign of Richard II of England was troubled from the beginning. Ships from France and Castile had raided the southern coast in 1377. England was afraid of an all-out invasion, and money was needed for ships and to build up defenses. Parliament authorized three poll, or head, taxes. Since all people were to pay the same amount, regardless of how wealthy they were, the tax was a much heavier burden on the common people and the poor. Their grumbling became louder and finally erupted in the Peasants' Revolt in 1381.

The causes of the revolt went far deeper than the tax. For hundreds of years the common people had been taught by the church and the nobility that their place in life had been ordained by God's divine will and that to try to rise in society was to go against God. The peasants began to challenge this idea. They were less content to spend their lives in backbreaking work to enrich their lords, who did no work at all. The Hundred Years' War had much to do with this. England was filled with thousands of men whose arrows had struck down French nobles at Crécy and Poitiers. Many of these soldiers had brought back wealth from the war and were unwilling to see it devoured by taxes.

The Black Death also helped prepare the way for the revolt. With so many poor people dead, the lords lacked enough men to harvest their crops. Labor was scarce, and landowners had to bid for the services of commoners. It would be too much to say that the English peasants in 1381 wanted equality, but at least they wanted life to be less unequal. One of their leaders, a priest named John Ball, said that men were equal because they all shared a common ancestor. He used a rhyme to make his point:

From his royal barge on the Thames River, England's King Richard II negotiates with peasant rebels on the shore.

When Adam delved and Eve span
    [spun cloth],
Where was then the gentleman?[86]

The March on London

The revolt began in southeast England and spread rapidly. Unlike the French Jacques, the rebels had specific reforms in mind, namely the lifting of the poll tax. Thousands marched on London, intending to force King Richard to meet their demands. They captured the Tower of London and murdered the archbishop of Canterbury. They forced the king, whose forces they far outnumbered, to meet them outside London.

The two sides met at Smithfield. The peasants' leader, Wat Tyler, who had once been a soldier in France, presented the rebels' demands. He spoke so rudely to Richard, however, that one of the king's men drew his sword and killed Tyler. The

Rebel leader Wat Tyler is killed by one of King Richard's men for speaking disrespectfully to his majesty during a meeting.

rebels started forward to avenge his death. Richard and his men might have been killed, but the fourteen-year-old king bravely rode alone and convinced the rebels to go away peacefully.

The revolt was broken, but it had nearly succeeded. It had a profound effect on both the nobility and the common people. The nobility, afraid of another revolt, took swift and brutal revenge, hanging anyone they thought had been a leader. Those peasants returned to their villages and farms, but they did not forget what they had almost accomplished. Perhaps they told their children that they might succeed where their parents had failed.

Thomas of Gloucester

Unhappily for Richard, this was the high point of his reign. His uncle, John of Gaunt, settled in Guyenne—first as Richard's lieutenant and later as duke—and no longer played a major role in

A youthful King Richard II bravely risks his life as he persuades a bloodthirsty crowd of rebels bent on vengeance to disperse.

Preaching for Equality

The notion that all people are equal was new in the fourteenth century. Thomas Walsingham's account of the preaching of John Ball is found in A. R. Myers's English Historical Documents:

"And continuing the sermon thus begun, he strove, by the words of the proverb that he had taken for his theme, to introduce and to prove that from the beginning all men were created equal by nature, and that servitude had been introduced by the unjust oppression of wicked men, against God's will; because, if it had pleased him to create serfs [slavelike peasants], surely in the beginning of the world he would have decreed who was to be a serf and who a lord. Let them consider, therefore, that a time was now given them by God, a time in which they might be able to lay aside the yoke of servitude, if they wished, and enjoy their hope for liberty. Wherefore they should be prudent men, and, with the love of a good husband-man tilling his field and uprooting and destroying the tares [weeds] which are wont [accustomed] to choke the grain, they should hasten to do the following things. First, they should kill the great lords of the kingdom; second, they should slay the lawyers, judges, and jurors of the country; finally they should root all those whom they knew to be likely to be harmful to the commonwealth in future. Thus they would obtain peace and security in the future, if, when the great ones had been removed, there were among them equal liberty and nobility and like dignity and power."

John Ball incited commoners to claim by violence their equality with the nobility.

English politics. Instead, the kingdom was controlled by a council elected by Parliament but dominated by Richard's uncle Thomas, duke of Gloucester, Edward III's youngest son.

Richard began to gather a group of supporters around him. It included Richard's chancellor, or secretary, Michael de la Pole, who could see that to continue the war with France would bankrupt the country. He wanted peace. The leading nobles, led by Gloucester, wanted war.

When Gloucester spoke against Pole's policy in Parliament in 1386, Richard threatened to turn to "our cousin, the King of France" for help.[87] Gloucester replied that if a king

> rashly in his insane counsels exercise his own peculiar desire, it is lawful for the lords and magnates to pluck down the king from his royal throne and to raise to the throne some very near kinsman of the royal house. The King of France is your chief enemy and the mortal foe of your realm. And if

he should set foot on your land, he would rather work to despoil you, seize your kingdom and drive you from your throne, than lend you helping hands. . . . Recall to your memory therefore how your grandfather King Edward III and your father Prince Edward worked untirely all their lives, in sweat and toil, in heat and cold, for the conquest of the realm of France, which was their hereditary right and is yours by succession after them.[88]

Richard gave in and dismissed Pole, but a year later, at the age of twenty, declared he had come of age and appointed a new council from among his supporters. But the forces of Gloucester defeated Richard's supporters at the Battle of Radcourt Bridge in 1387, and the king was placed under the control of five Lords Appellant, who included Gloucester and Henry, earl of Derby, oldest son of John of Gaunt.

The French Royal Uncles

In France, also, a council was set up to govern in the name of the young Charles VI. It was controlled by the king's uncles, the dukes of Burgundy, Anjou, and Berry. Berry and Anjou found other interests, however, and the country was really ruled by one man, Philip the Bold, duke of Burgundy—the same Philip who had, at age ten, fought beside his father, King John, at Poitiers. Philip became unpopular with the people of France because of the high taxes he imposed to put down a revolt in Flanders and to build ships for an invasion of England, which never took place.

Charles VI, like his cousin Richard, eventually grew impatient to rule on his

Thomas, duke of Gloucester, respectfully greets his royal nephew, King Richard II. The duke dominated England's ruling council before Richard was old enough to rule.

King Charles VI of France and his queen, Isabeau of Bavaria.

own. In 1388, prompted by his brother Louis, duke of Orléans, and his wife, Isabeau of Bavaria, he dismissed his uncles and formed his own council. The council was no more popular with the people than Philip the Bold had been. Taxes continued to be high, much of the money going for tournaments, feasts, dances, and other revelry by the free-spending king and his brother.

Little money was available for war, either in England or in France. Charles's council favored a policy of peace, and although the English barons talked of war, they knew they could not afford it. Negotiations began in 1388 at Leulinghen, and a three-year truce between France and England was signed in June 1389.

Charles VI's Character

Just when the two countries appeared headed toward a permanent peace, the government of France was thrown into confusion by the illness of the king. Charles VI, at twenty-four, was "no more than a big boy, carefree, erratic, and slack," a "feeble soul, who has rightly been called

a perpetual minor."[89] After years of being pulled this way and that by everyone around him, his mind gave way in 1392. He began to have periods of insanity. At first he would simply sit staring into space. Later his behavior grew more bizarre. He would run down the halls of the palace in his nightshirt, howling like a wolf. He would allow no one to touch him, claiming he was made of glass and might shatter.

The royal uncles used the king's illness to take power back from the council, but they did not want to renew the war. For one thing, Philip the Bold, duke of Flanders as well as Burgundy, wanted no interruption of the wool trade. Negotiations went on. Richard's representatives, amazingly, yielded on the question of absolute sovereignty of Guyenne, which Edward III had demanded for fifty years. Then, the old problem arose. Would Richard do full homage, requiring him to come to the aid of the king of France in all cases, or limited homage? The talks almost stopped.

Richard would not let them. He wanted peace and closer contact with France. He had begun to rule in his own name in 1389, although the barons still had great power. He was fascinated by the

The marriage of King Richard II and the child-princess Isabella, daughter of France's King Charles VI.

glitter and splendor of the French court where, not only the king, but also the royal dukes, tried to outdo one another. While France had serious problems, Perroy wrote,

> From the outside it appeared still powerful. . . . All the princes vied with one another in luxury and prodigality [excessive wastefulness]. Every one of them insisted on having his own motto, his own badge, his own livery, even his own order of chivalry. All the court purveyors [suppliers], drapers, tapestry makers, jewelers, brokers, feathered their nests. . . . The monarchy of the Valois lived on its reputation in past centuries and profited by its acquired momentum, which was far superior to the strength actually at its disposal.[90]

Richard tried to solve the problem of Guyenne by making his uncle, John of Gaunt, the duke. With the king of England no longer holding the title, the problem of homage would be solved. The lords of Guyenne objected, afraid that Guyenne would be absorbed back into France.

A Royal Wedding

Richard had another plan. His wife, Anne of Bohemia, had died in 1394. Richard had long wanted to meet Charles and now proposed that he should marry Charles's daughter, Isabella, although he was nearly thirty and she was only six. In October Richard went to Calais to meet his child bride and his new father-in-law. Splendid festivities took place. The two kings' uncles swore eternal friendship. Richard promised to support the French policy elsewhere in Europe, even backing the French pope.

The marriage and Richard's promises were extremely unpopular in England, especially the part of the agreement that said the French would support Richard "against all manner of people who owe him any obedience and also to aid and sustain him with all their power against any of

A King Becomes a Tyrant

As he grew older King Richard II of England grew suspicious and more tyrannical. This excerpt from the Continuatio Eulogii Historiarum (A Continuation of the Praise of Histories), *printed in Myers's* English Historical Documents *describes how he ensured his subjects' "loyalty":*

"Then the king called together his councillors and the archbishop and bishops at Nottingham, and said that he could not safely ride through the kingdom on account of the hatred of the men of London and the seventeen adjacent shires, and therefore he wished to destroy them with the army that he would assemble unless they would find him a pledge of good behavior. Therefore, they ordered that the city and each shire should collect a great sum of money and offer it to him as a pledge of peace; and this was done. They ordered moreover that archbishops, bishops, abbots, priors, lords, and commons in the cities and towns should affix their seals to blank charters . . . in which the king intended later on, as it is said, to write this sentence: 'as we have gravely offended your majesty in days gone by, we give ourselves and our good to you, and the promptings of your will.'"

his subjects."[91] When the leading barons began to unite in protest, Richard acted quickly. He had the leaders arrested and killed, including his uncle, the duke of Gloucester, who was strangled with a towel in his Calais prison cell.

Richard now became a tyrant. "The king began to keep state [hold court] far

The duke of Gloucester is arrested and led to a ship waiting to take him to Calais for imprisonment.

King Richard hands over his crown and scepter to Henry, duke of Lancaster. Henry became king and Richard a condemned prisoner.

more extravagantly than any king of England had ever done," wrote Froissart. "At this time, there was nobody in England, however great, that dared speak out about the actions or intentions of the king."[92] Those who did were executed.

Richard began to fear his cousin Henry, who would inherit the huge estate of his father, John of Gaunt. When Henry and the duke of Norfolk quarreled in 1398 and decided to settle matters by combat, Richard stepped in, stopped the fight, and banished both from England. Henry fled to France. That same year John of Gaunt died. Richard confiscated most of the huge duchy of Lancaster, dividing it among his friends.

A Not-Too-Fond Farewell

Richard II, because of his harsh rule and the favor he showed toward the French, was unpopular in England. This was reflected in the Chronicle of Adam of Usk:

"And now, Richard, fare thee well!, king indeed (if I may call thee so) most mighty; for after death all might praise thee, hadst thou, with the help of God and thy people, so ordered thy deeds as to deserve such praise. But, though well endowed as Solomon, though fair as Absalom, though glorious as Ahasuerus, though a builder excellent as the great Belus, yet, like Chosroes, King of Persia, who was delivered into the hands of Heraclius, didst thou in the midst of thy glory, as Fortune turned her wheel, fall most miserably into the hand of duke Henry, amid the smothered curses of thy people."

Henry Takes the Throne

Henry vowed to regain his inheritance. In the spring of 1399, when Richard was away in Ireland, he landed in England with a small armed force. The barons, tired of Richard's rule, hurried to support Henry. When Richard returned he was thrown into prison. In September Henry came to Parliament. He showed Richard's ring—the sign of office the king had received at his coronation. He said that Richard had willingly surrendered it. He presented a document in which, Henry said, Richard confessed that he was unworthy to rule and renounced his throne. Henry claimed it and was crowned Henry IV, the first of the Lancastrian branch of the Plantagenets to rule England.

Richard was moved to a castle far away from London, but Henry could not afford to let him remain alive. Richard was allowed to starve to death. He had tried to impose on England the absolute monarchy of France. If he had succeeded, France might have gained dominance over England. "His failure was a personal tragedy," wrote McKisack, "but his success would have been the tragedy of a nation [England]."[93]

France feared the war would resume since Henry had opposed Richard's pro-French policy. The king of England, however, was in no position to invade France. He had enough trouble at home. Some barons who had supported Richard began plotting against Henry. The Scots took advantage of the internal struggle in England and began raiding the northern border. The Welsh rebelled for the first time in more than a hundred years.

Henry, duke of Lancaster, is crowned Henry IV, king of England, after forcing Richard's resignation from the throne.

Burgundy and Armagnac

A united France now probably could have pushed the English out of both Calais and Guyenne, but there was little unity in the French court. Philip of Burgundy and Louis, duke of Orléans, vied for control of the king, and this split the country into two factions. "No sharing between them was possible," Perroy wrote. "Very soon they reached a point where they opposed each other in everything."[94] When Philip died in 1404, the situation grew even worse. The new duke of Burgundy, John the Fearless, was even more ambitious than his father.

Louis and John became bitter enemies. Their followers fought in the streets of Paris. Finally, John tried to end the conflict once and for all. One night in November 1407 Louis was ambushed and murdered by John's men. John wept at Louis's funeral, but when his role was revealed, he cried out, "I did it; the Devil tempted me" and fled to Flanders.[95] Civil war had begun.

France was divided into two armed sides, the Burgundians, whose duke was John, and the Armagnacs, followers of the slain Louis. The Armagnacs took their name from the count of Armagnac, whose son had married Louis's daughter. The Armagnacs consisted mostly of the wealthier merchants, the leading nobles (except those in John's territories), and most of the royal family. The Burgundians were supported by most of the merchants, the universities, and the citizens of Paris.

An Open Door to War

John of Burgundy quickly regained control. He returned to Paris in 1408, claiming that Louis had been so corrupt that murdering him was actually an act of justice. He won the loyalty of the people of Paris by promising reforms and relief from taxes. The Armagnacs reacted by raising an army and blockading Paris. John then

England's King Henry IV involved his troops in France's internal struggle and thus opened the door for the Hundred Years' War to resume.

opened the door for the war between England and France to resume. In 1411 he invited Henry IV to send an army from England to help him.

Henry did not want to commit all his troops. He sent only eight hundred men-at-arms and two thousand archers. They landed at Calais in October, helped John break the blockade, and quickly went home.

The Armagnacs now tried to outbid the Burgundians for Henry's help. In 1412 they offered to restore Guyenne as it had been under the Treaty of Brétigny. Henry sent them a larger force commanded by his son, the duke of Clarence. By the time it arrived the Armagnacs had been forced to accept a truce. That did not stop Clarence, who marched into the heart of France, burning and looting along the way. He stopped only when the Armagnacs promised him a huge cash payment.

Now, too late, John the Fearless realized his mistake in allowing English troops into France. He called the Estates to Paris in 1413 and asked for taxes to defend against an English invasion. When the Estates protested, John urged the people of Paris to riot. The mob got out of hand, attacking not only the Armagnacs, but also anyone who seemed wealthy. The leading merchants and many of the nobles who had supported John now turned against him. In August 1413 John retreated to Burgundy, where he would spend the next five years.

The Armagnacs were back in control, but the damage was done. Henry IV had died in March and his son, Henry V, was on the throne. The greed of the English barons had been aroused. They wanted war and now had a king who was ready to give it to them.

7 Henry V and Agincourt

In 1413 England had a new king, Henry V, with the same love of war, singleness of purpose, and skill as a general as his great-grandfather, Edward III. At the same time, France had an insane monarch, Charles VI, and was deeply divided by the struggle between the Burgundians and the Armagnacs. This combination paved the way for England's greatest triumphs of the Hundred Years' War and France's greatest humiliations.

Henry V reigned only nine years but, because of his accomplishments in France, has been remembered as perhaps the most glorious of all English kings. He has been called a "princely hero."[96] Another

The coronation of Henry V as king of England in 1413. Henry reigned for only nine years but is remembered as one of England's greatest monarchs.

historian said that, of all the kings, "he alone inspired at once the admiration and affection of his people."[97] One reason for Henry's reputation is that he died at the very height of his fame, before he had any chance to lose what he had gained.

Henry had several reasons to renew the war with France. First, with the country at peace, hundreds of unemployed soldiers had become outlaws and were a menace to everyone. A war would give them honest work. Second, the nobility, whose chief pastime and occupation was war, had not had one for a generation. Third, France was deeply divided and appeared ripe for the taking. Also, Henry was personally drawn toward war with France. He was "obeying the traditions of his forebears as most Englishmen expected him to do, and he had seen what had happened to Richard II who had gone against that tradition."[98]

Bargaining with Both Sides

Henry was not only a proven soldier, but also a clever politician. He wanted to make it look like the French resumed the war. Both factions in France—Burgundians and Armagnacs—were seeking his help.

From Wildness to Piety

Tradition says that Henry V was wild as a youth but gave up his former ways on becoming king. This transformation was described in The Brut Chronicle *and printed in A. R. Myers's* English Historical Documents:

"And at once [Henry] commanded all his people who were parties to his misgovernance before that time, and all his household, to come before him. And when they heard that, they were full glad, for they supposed that he would have promoted them into great offices, and that they would stand in great favour and trust with him, and be nearest of counsel, as they were before that time. And trusting thereupon, they were the homelier [familiar] and bolder unto him, and did not dread him at all, insomuch that when they were come before him, some of them winked at him, and some smiled, and thus they made foolish grimaces unto him, many of them. But for all that, the prince kept his countenance very serious towards them, and said to them: 'Sirs, you are the people that I have cherished and maintained in riot and wild governance, and here I give you all in commandment and charge you that from this day forward you forsake all misgovernance and live according to the laws of Almighty God and the laws of our land. And whoever does the contrary, I make faithful promise to God that he shall be truly punished according to the law, without any favour or grace.' And he charged them, on pain of death, that they should never give him comfort nor counsel to fall to riot any more."

From the Burgundians Henry demanded all the territory granted England in the Treaty of Brétigny, plus recognition as king of France. From the Armagnacs he demanded a marriage between himself and a daughter of Charles VI, with an enormous dowry—a payment by the bride's family to the groom. In fact, he had no intention of accepting anything. He wanted war and had been preparing for it for a year. At last the French realized that nothing would satisfy Henry and broke off negotiations in February 1415. Henry used this as his excuse to invade France.

The English army sailed on August 10, landing in Normandy. Henry intended to conquer Normandy and then march up the Seine River to Paris. His first target was the port city of Harfleur. The city surrendered, but only after a siege lasting more than a month. With winter approaching and with many of his troops dead from disease, Henry could not head for Paris. Instead of returning to England from Harfleur, however, he decided to march 160 miles north to Calais.

The French had assembled an army far larger than Henry's and came after him. The English did not realize they were being pursued. When they tried to use the same ford over the Somme River that Edward III had used sixty-nine years before, they found it blocked by French troops. Henry headed east and was finally able to cross the river at Béthincourt, but the French army still stood between the English and Calais.

The Battle of Agincourt

Henry knew he would have to fight. On October 24 the English took up a strong defensive position near the village of Agincourt. The next morning both armies prepared for battle. It had rained all night, and the recently plowed field between them was muddy. Henry hoped the French would charge so that he could use his archers as the English had done at Crécy and Poitiers. The French had learned from their defeats, however, and stood still. Finally, Henry ordered his archers to advance until they were within range and then begin shooting.

The French, under a hail of arrows, had no choice but to attack. The mounted men-at-arms came first. Their horses bogged down in the mud and were easy targets for the English. The dismounted men-at-arms came next. They, too, were slowed down by the mud, and many were killed before they reached the English lines.

At last the French reached the English line and almost broke through. Henry ordered his archers to drop their bows and help the English men-at-arms. The archers had little or no armor and could move

Henry V surrounded by his war regalia.

more easily through the knee-deep mud. They got behind the Frenchmen and stabbed them through the joints in their armor. Some of the French were simply knocked over and drowned in the mud, unable to get up. An eyewitness later wrote:

For when some of them slain at the start of the engagement fell in front, such was the indisciplined violence and pressure of the host behind that the living fell on the dead, and others falling on the living were killed in turn; and so in the three places where there was a concentration of forces, the piles of dead and those crushed in between grew so much that our men climbed on these heaps which grew higher than a man and slew those below with swords, axes, and other weapons.[99]

Before the Battle

One of the most famous speeches in all English literature was written by William Shakespeare. King Henry encourages his soldiers just before the Battle of Agincourt, fought on the feast day of Saints Crispin and Crispian, in Henry V. *This excerpt is from* The Living Shakespeare:

He that shall live this day, and see old age,
Will yearly on the vigil [day before the saint's day]
    feast his neighbors,
And say "To-morrow is Saint Crispian":
Then will he strip his sleeve and show his scars,
and say "These wounds I had on Crispin's day.
Old men forget; yet all shall be forgot,
But he'll remember with advantages
What feats he did that day: then shall our names,
Familiar in his mouth as household words,
Harry the king, Bedford and Exeter,
Warwick and Talbot, Salisbury and Gloucester,
Be in their flowing cups freshly remember'd.
This story shall the good man teach his son;
And Crispin Crispian shall ne'er go by,
From this day to the ending of the world,
But we in it shall be remembered;
We few, we happy few, we band of brothers;
For he to-day that sheds his blood with me
shall be my brother; be he ne'er so vile,
This day shall gentle his condition:
And gentlemen in England now a-bed
shall think themselves accursed they were not here,
And hold their manhoods cheap while any speaks
That fought with us upon Saint Crispin's day."

A memorial of Henry V and his warriors at the Battle of Agincourt. This battle, although not unlike other raids before it, stands out because it made the English seem invincible.

Then, with the battle almost won, Henry committed one of those acts that shows a darker side and dims the picture of him as a gallant hero. The English had sent their prisoners to the rear, where the baggage was stored. When some French peasants began to raid the baggage, Henry ordered that all the prisoners be killed, except for the most valuable. These unarmed men were "sticked with daggers, brained with poleaxes, slain with malles [mallets]."[100]

The writers of the time, both English and French, condemned him, and modern historian Desmond Seward called it "a particularly nasty atrocity."[101] Harold Hutchison, in his biography, called the killing of the prisoners an example of Henry's tendency toward "pointless ruthlessness" and says that under Henry, "warfare had no panoply [covering] of mercy to hide its naked brutality."[102]

After the battle the English completed their march to Calais, loaded with plunder and about fifteen hundred prisoners. After a brief stay in Calais Henry returned to England in triumph. The Battle of Agincourt appeared to be "only one raid more after so many like it."[103] Its importance was that it added to the growing idea that the English were invincible. Not only the English, but also the French themselves, were coming to think that a single English soldier was worth many of the enemy. This concept would carry England to victories in future wars, both in Europe and all over the world as the British Empire spread.

Henry's Second Invasion

Henry persuaded Parliament to equip a new army of ten thousand men to launch another attack on France. The army landed in Normandy on August 1, 1417. This time it was not just another raid. Henry planned to conquer Normandy and use it as a base to conquer the rest of France.

His timing was perfect. The Armagnacs were losing their power. Several of their leaders had been captured at Agincourt. French king Charles VI's oldest sons, Louis and John, had died, leaving Charles, an unpromising lad of fourteen, as dauphin. Both the king and the new dauphin were controlled by the count of Armagnac. Even Queen Isabeau was gone. After a quarrel with her son and the count of Armagnac, her allowance was cut and she was shipped off to Tours. She later escaped and joined John the Fearless.

Later in 1417 John sent a Burgundian army to surround Paris, hoping to pressure the city into surrender. On May 29, 1418, the citizens rebelled and opened the city gates to the Burgundian troops. An eyewitness wrote that "the people, bitterly inflamed against the confederates [Armagnacs], went through all the houses of Paris hunting for them. All that they found, of whatever rank . . . they hauled them out into the streets and killed them at once without mercy, with heavy axes and other weapons."[104] The dauphin managed to escape, but the count of Armagnac was killed.

While the French squabbled, Henry conquered Normandy. Caen fell on September 20, 1417, and more than two thousand civilians were massacred to serve as a lesson to other cities. Henry's brutal strategy worked. Other cities quickly surrendered, and the English were free to attack the capital of Normandy, Rouen.

The Siege of Rouen

The siege of Rouen, which began on July 29, 1418, was one of the most cruel in history. The city was too strong to be taken by force, so the English decided to starve it into surrender. The siege dragged on into the winter. An English soldier named John Page left this description:

> They [the people of Rouen] had no meat save horse meat. They also ate both dogs and cats, both rats and mice. . . . A morsel of bread as small as the half of one's hand was worth a French franc, and it was hard to find. . . . And then they took to eating rotten food and any vegetable peelings they could find—they even ate dock [weed] roots. . . . If a child was dying the mother would give it no bread—instead of sharing it with the little they had left, she would hide it far from the bread-bin so that the child could not find it, and she could eat it by herself in secret. Neither would a child share with its mother—it preferred to eat by itself. All love and kindness were forgotten.[105]

The city finally surrendered on January 19, 1419. The people cheered Henry, grateful the siege was over, but "many of them were mere skin and bones with hollow eyes and pinched noses."[106] Other Norman towns fell to Henry quickly, and by the end of the year he was master of the entire province and was within striking distance of Paris.

English soldiers plant their banner on the walls of Rouen, the capital of Normandy, after besieging it for six months.

The Murder of John the Fearless

John the Fearless of Burgundy was so alarmed at Henry's successes that he had even begun negotiating with the hated Armagnacs. The Armagnacs, however, hated John more than they feared Henry. The dauphin and the duke, with a few attendants each, met at the center of a bridge at Montereau in September 1419. According to one account:

> When the Duke of Burgundy saw the Dauphin, he knelt down and did the reverence and honor that was appropriate and said, "Sir, I am come at your command; you know the desolation of the kingdom and of your domain: pay heed to its restoration. As for me, I am ready and prepared to expose my body and goods for this end, and those of my vassals, subject, and allies." Then, they say, the Dauphin raised his hat, thanked him, and told him to rise: and as the Duke rose, the Dauphin made a sign to those who were with him: and then the Lord Tanneguy du Chastel came near the duke and pushed him by the shoulders, saying to him, "Die!" and struck him with an axe on the head, and so he slew him in this way.[107]

The assassination of John the Fearless made it impossible for the Burgundians and Armagnacs to unite against Henry. Instead, John's son Philip the Good formed an alliance with the king of England, promising to help him conquer the rest of the country. "The murder at Montereau had so blinded Burgundian Frenchmen," Hutchison wrote, "that in pursuit of a personal vendetta [revenge], they were now prepared to sell France to the invader."[108]

Revenge for a Murder

The murder of John the Fearless, duke of Burgundy, by agents of the dauphin on the bridge at Montereau in 1419 destroyed any hope for unity in France. Jean Juvenal des Ursins's description is found in English Historical Documents:

"When the new Duke of Burgundy, named Philip, learnt of the death of his father, he was very grieved and angry and not without cause: and he assembled his council to know what he ought to do. Moreover he sent to the King of England to treat [negotiate] of peace, even more fully than his father had offered: and in this hope truce was made between the Duke of Burgundy, in the name of the king whom he abused, and the King of England. And their people considered themselves as all of the same party, English and Burgundians, to make mortal war on the Dauphin and those who supported to him, to avenge themselves for this death."

The Treaty of Troyes

Philip joined Charles VI and Queen Isabeau, who had returned to her husband after the Burgundians took Paris, in Troyes in March 1420. There they met with Henry's representatives. In April the Treaty of Troyes was drawn up. Henry was to marry Charles's daughter, Catherine, and receive a huge dowry. Charles would remain king of France, but Henry would be next in line for the throne. Because of Charles's mental illness, Henry would act as regent. The dauphin was disinherited, based on Isabeau's claiming that Charles was not her son's real father. The duke of Burgundy was to help Henry conquer the rest of France. Historian Desmond Seward called the Treaty of Troyes "one of the greatest humiliations in French history, comparable to that of 1940 (when France surrendered to Adolf Hitler's Germany)."[109]

In May Henry journeyed to Troyes to meet his future father-in-law. The feeble-minded Charles did not seem to know who

Henry V receives the hand of Princess Catherine of France in marriage as part of the agreement made in the Treaty of Troyes. The treaty also made Henry heir to France's throne.

his visitor was. Henry and Catherine were married on June 2, 1420, and a witness wrote: "It was plainly to be seen that King Henry was desperately in love with her" and that Catherine "had longed passionately to be espoused to King Henry."[110]

The French and English knights wanted to hold a grand tournament to celebrate the marriage, but Henry had other ideas. He said:

> I beg my lord the King whose daughter I have married, and all his servants, and I command all my own servants that tomorrow morning we all of us be ready to go and besiege Sens, where my lord the King's [Charles] enemies [the Armagnacs] are. There we may all tilt and joust and prove our daring and courage, for there is no finer act of courage in the world than to punish evildoers so that poor people can live.[111]

Accordingly, Catherine spent her honeymoon camped outside Sens, which fell to Henry and Philip the Good on June 11.

Finally, on September 20, Philip and Henry made a ceremonial entry into Paris, which would be under combined English-Burgundian rule for the next eighteen years. Henry spent Christmas in splendid style while King Charles, now ignored by all but his most faithful servants, was "poorly and meanly served."[112]

Henry and Catherine went to England at the end of January 1421. Henry had been absent from his kingdom for three and a half years. In April he received news that his younger brother, the duke of Clarence, had been killed and the English defeated at Baugé in Normandy. It was the first real battle of the war that had been won by the French. Although not very important from a military point of view, it showed the French that the English could be defeated.

Henry Returns to France

Henry hurried back to France in June. Paris was being threatened from three sides by the dauphin's forces. The English quickly captured several cities, and Henry was determined to avenge his brother's death. When the castle of Rougemont was captured, every defender was hanged.

Henry now turned toward Meaux, the center of the dauphin's forces, about forty miles from Paris. This important city controlled any approach to Paris from the east. The siege was hard for both those inside and outside Paris. Constant rain and bitter cold caused more disease than usual. Henry himself became ill. His only good news was that Catherine had, on December 6, 1421, given birth to a son, Henry of Windsor.

Meaux surrendered on March 9, 1422. Henry showed little mercy. A trumpeter who had mocked him from the city walls was beheaded. Other soldiers who had displayed a donkey and then shouted to the English to come rescue their king were sent to the most foul dungeons Henry could find.

The victory of Meaux was to prove costly. Henry's illness, probably dysentery, had grown worse. He joined Catherine in Paris in May but was able to get little rest. In June, although very sick, Henry was determined to lead an army to nearby Cosne. But he was unable to stay in the saddle and had to be carried back to the castle of Vincennes, just three miles from Paris. Henry

Henry V died without ever seeing his son who became Henry VI of England as well as Henri II of France, the only Plantagenet to rule both realms.

knew he was dying. He made his brother John, duke of Bedford, regent of France and guardian of the son he would never see. Another brother, Humphrey, duke of Gloucester, was to be regent in England. Henry died on September 1, 1422, only thirty-five years old.

Two months later King Charles VI of France died, alone and almost forgotten. His wife did not even attend his funeral. Neither did his son nor his nephews. The duke of Bedford was there, however, and took the opportunity to proclaim his eight-month-old nephew to be both King Henry VI of England and King Henri II of France. After almost a hundred years the dream of Edward III—a Plantagenet on the thrones of both England and France—had been realized.

Chapter

8 The Duke, the Dauphin, and the Maid

The thirteen years after the death of Henry V in 1422 saw the start of a long decline in the fortunes of the English in France. Their gains began to melt away, despite the able administration of Henry's brother, the duke of Bedford. With the help of Joan of Arc, France would once more be united under a French king.

Charles VII of France. As the dauphin, Charles had been stripped of his right to the French throne by the Treaty of Troyes.

In 1422, however, France was far from united. Northern France was divided into three distinct areas. The first, including Normandy and Brittany, was directly ruled by the duke of Bedford, acting for the infant King Henry VI of England, who was known in France as King Henri II. The second consisted of Flanders in the far north and Burgundy in the east and was ruled by Philip the Good, who was duke over both. The third, the area north of the Loire River, including Paris, was controlled jointly by the English, under Bedford, and the Burgundians, under Philip.

The remainder of France, larger and more wealthy than all the rest combined, consisted of the southern third, except for Guyenne. This large territory remained loyal to the dauphin and continued to fight for him against the English.

Character of the Dauphin

Southern, or dauphinist, France, with Henry V dead, should have been strong enough to reconquer the country. The character of the dauphin was the chief reason why it could not. Charles was now nineteen and not an inspiring leader. Perroy wrote:

One could scarcely imagine a prince less fitted to evoke enthusiasm, defend a cause in peril and play the part of a leader and later of king. Physically and mentally, Charles was a weakling, a graceless degenerate. He was stunted and puny, with a blank face in which scared, shifty, sleepy eyes, peering out on either side of a big, long nose, failed to animate his harsh, unpleasant features.[113]

He was controlled by others most of his life. He was not a soldier and "didn't love war at all, if he could avoid it."[114]

Philip the Good of Burgundy was in a difficult position. If he gave his entire support to the English, they would rule all of France. Philip was proud enough not to want that. Still, he could not forgive Charles and the Armagnacs for the murder of his father, John the Fearless. As a result, he played a waiting game.

The Duke of Bedford

Bedford was a most outstanding leader. Seward wrote that he was "an excellent soldier, administrator and diplomatist, and possessed a rugged determination."[115] He loved the French and attempted to win their loyalty by ruling fairly. To make his alliance with Burgundy stronger, Bedford married Philip's sister, Anne. Because of his ability, the seven years after Henry V's death were some of the most successful for England in the entire war.

In 1423 a dauphinist army besieged Cravant near the western border of Burgundy. Bedford's chief commander, the earl of Salisbury, led an army to relieve the

John, duke of Bedford and Henry V's brother, ably and fairly ruled France as regent for the infant Henry VI.

city and, on July 29, won a complete victory. In August 1424, in a larger battle, Bedford's army defeated a much larger dauphinist force at Verneuil in Normandy and took the duke of Alençon prisoner.

The Battle of Verneuil "was seen as a second Agincourt."[116] The loss of Alençon and his army left the dauphin no real fighting force. But, just when a major campaign might have ended the war, the alliance between England and Burgundy was threatened by Bedford's brother, the duke of Gloucester. Gloucester, whom Perroy called a "scatterbrain," had married Countess Jacqueline of Hainault.[117] In an attempt to win her disputed inheritance, Gloucester led a small army to Hainault, only to be quickly chased home by Duke Philip of Burgundy, who wanted Jacqueline's lands for himself. Burgundy thought

The Attack on Orléans

English and French knights battle at Verneuil. The English won, capturing the duke of Alençon and leaving the dauphin without a fighting force.

Bedford had aided his brother. He threatened to break off the alliance and begin negotiations with the dauphin. Only Anne of Burgundy was able to restore peace between her brother and her husband.

In 1425 Bedford was forced to return to England to settle a quarrel between Gloucester and Chancellor Henry Beaufort, who had become the real power in England, although Gloucester was officially regent. Gloucester had tried to get the Londoners to rebel against Beaufort, and a civil war nearly broke out. "If you tarry [delay], we shall put this land in peril with a battle," Beaufort wrote to Bedford. "Such a brother you have here." [118] Bedford was in England from December 1425 until March 1427 to make peace, months he could have spent making war in France.

The dauphin was in no position to take advantage of Bedford's absence. Instead of fighting the English or Burgundians, the dauphinists were fighting among each other for control of Charles. When Bedford returned to France, he saw the weakness of the dauphinists and decided on a major campaign to end the war. He needed a major city on the Loire to use as a base. He chose Orléans, the key to central France and the city "whose fall would have the most resounding effect." [119] The siege began in October 1428 under the command of the earl of Salisbury. The English forces were so small—about four thousand—and the city so large that they could not surround it, but circled it with patrols.

Both sides felt that, if Orléans fell, the dauphin's cause was lost. The defenders of Orléans begged Philip of Burgundy to rescue them, but he replied only by removing the small number of Burgundian troops. Charles himself spoke openly of fleeing to Dauphiné or even to Scotland. But just when it seemed as if England would triumph, France received what her people have always considered a miracle—the sudden appearance of Joan of Arc.

Joan of Arc

Joan remains one of the most unusual characters in history. The English called her a witch. Bedford wrote that she was "a disciple of the fiend [Satan]." [120] Some writers say she was divinely inspired; others say she was insane. Her admirers say she saved

France. Most historians say she had little effect on the war. Even the dauphin Charles, whom she placed on the throne, was unsure of her and perhaps not too sorry when she died.

Joan was born about 1412, the daughter of a well-to-do farmer. From the age of thirteen she heard "voices" of God and various saints. In 1428 these voices told her that it was her destiny to lead the dauphin to victory. She appeared before the region's dauphinist leader, Robert de Baudricourt, claiming, "Despite his enemies, the Dauphin will be made king; and it is I who will take him to his coronation."[121]

Impressed, Baudricourt sent her to Chinon, where Charles's court was at the time. She immediately recognized Charles, even though he had deliberately dressed plainly and stood among a crowd of courtiers. "Very noble Lord Dauphin," she said, "I am come and am sent by God, to bring succour [help] to you and to your kingdom."[122] Later, in a private talk with Charles, Joan told him it was her mission to lift the siege of Orléans and to lead Charles to be crowned in Reims.

Charles was desperate enough to allow her to try. Joan sent a defiant letter to Bedford, saying:

Joan of Arc was a unique historical figure. Some thought her possessed or insane; others saw her as a saint and a savior.

> You, Duke of Bedford, who call yourself regent of the kingdom of France. . . acknowledge the summons of the King of Heaven, and render up to the Maid who is here sent by God, the King of Heaven, the keys of all the good towns you have here taken and violated in France. She is come here by God's will to reclaim the royal blood. . . . King of England, if you do not do so I am chief-of-war, and in whatever place I reach your people in France, I will make them quit it, willy-nilly. . . . If you will not believe the news sent to you by God and the Maid, we will strike into whatever place we find you, and make such great "hay-hay" [ruckus] that none so great has been in France for a thousand years. . . . You, Duke of Bedford . . . make answer if you wish to make peace in the city of Orléans; or if you do not do so, may you be reminded of it by your very great injuries.[123]

The Maid and the Dauphin

Chronicler Jean de Wavrin, who was a Burgundian and not at all fond of Joan of Arc, wrote this description of her arrival at the dauphin's court. It is found in English Historical Documents:

"And the maid was, at her coming, in very poor estate; and she was about two months in the house of the king, whom she many times admonished [counseled] by her speeches, as she had been instructed, to give her troops and aid, and she would repel and drive away his enemies, and exalt his name, enlarging his lordships, certifying that she had had a sufficient revelation concerning this; but whatever she could say at this beginning neither the king nor those of his council put much faith in her words or admonitions. And she was then considered at court only as one deranged and deluded, because she boasted herself as able to achieve so great an enterprise, which seemed to the great princes a thing impossible. . . . Nevertheless, after the maid had remained a good space at the king's court in the state that I have mentioned, she was brought forward and aided, and she raised a standard [flag] whereon she had painted the figure and representation of Our Lord Jesus Christ; indeed, all her words were full of the name of God, wherefore a great part of those who saw her and heard her speak, like fools, had great belief that she was inspired by God as she said."

Joan of Arc is introduced to Charles VII.

In early April 1429 four thousand troops set out for Orléans. Joan had convinced Charles to let her accompany the expedition, and he even had a suit of armor made for her.

The Relief of Orléans

The first part of the army reached Orléans on April 29, and Joan rode triumphantly into the city, accompanied by the captain of its defenders, Jean Dunois. The main body of troops arrived on May 3. Less than a week later the outnumbered English retreated.

Charles VII, in sheer desperation, allowed Joan of Arc to lead a force against the English at Orléans in 1429.

This portrait of the Maid of Orléans emphasizes her saintliness. She officially entered the canon, or list, of Roman Catholic saints in 1920.

Some of Charles's advisers wanted to march immediately on Paris, but Joan convinced him that the second part of her mission should be fulfilled. A large army set out on June 29 for what was expected to be a dangerous march to Reims, which was in the heart of country held by the English. Instead, the people of the towns, "feeling that the wind was veering, and with no desire to fight," opened their gates to Charles.[124]

Charles and Joan reached Reims on July 16, and the dauphin was formally crowned King Charles VII on the eighteenth. Joan stood beside him, holding her banner that showed Jesus "sitting in judgment among the clouds in the sky; and with him an angel painted holding a *fleur d'lis* in his hand."[125] Now, for the first time, Joan called Charles king rather than dauphin.

The coronation was the peak of Joan's career. By marching to Reims instead of Paris, Charles had given Bedford a chance to gather his forces. In September Charles's army reached Paris, and Joan herself led the attack, which failed. In October she failed to take the town of La Charité. The feeling that she was unbeatable was shattered. Charles disbanded his army and agreed to a truce that was to last until April 1430.

Joan's Capture, Trial, and Death

When the truce ended, Philip of Burgundy sent an army to besiege Compiègne, north of Paris. Charles sent Joan to try to lift the siege. On May 24, during a raid against the Burgundians, Joan was plucked off her horse by a Burgundian knight. The English and Burgundians were "much more excited than if they captured 500 fighting men, for they had never been so afraid of any captain or commander in war as they had been of the Maid." [126]

In November Joan was moved to Rouen, and her trial on charges of heresy [breaking God's laws] began on February 21, 1431. She was found guilty of, among other things, heresy, sorcery, and wearing men's clothing. Her judges, mostly French and Burgundian, handed her over to the English authorities under the earl of Warwick, and she was burned at the stake on May 30. She was only nineteen years old. Charles VII had made no attempt to help her.

Joan of Arc's immediate impact on the war was slight. Her successes, capture, and

Joan of Arc was burned at the stake as a witch in 1431 at Rouen. Many considered her a martyr for her faith.

execution failed to cause much excitement outside the areas in which they took place. Within a short time Bedford succeeded in regaining most of the lost territory. Yet, Joan had reinforced the lesson France had learned—namely that the English could be beaten. This knowledge gave France new hope and brought the end of the war nearer.

Henri II Crowned

Bedford tried to offset Joan's accomplishments by bringing the nine-year-old Henri II (Henry VI of England) to Paris to be crowned. The ceremony took place in the cathedral of Notre Dame on December 16, 1431. The coronation banquet turned into a riot. "The common people of Paris had gone into the hall early in the morning," wrote an observer of the time, "some of them to look, others to guzzle or to steal food or other things besides."[127] When Henry returned to England, "he had not gained one more partisan [follower] or stirred enthusiasm among his own supporters."[128]

The English began to lose ground in 1432. Chartres was lost in March. In the summer Bedford tried to regain momen-

---

France Is Reunited

The Treaty of Arras sealed the fate of the English in France by uniting the French and ending the alliance between England and Burgundy. Jean de Wavrin's account of the Congress of Arras in 1435 is found in English Historical Documents:

"So on 5th September, after taking leave of the Duke and Duchess of Burgundy, the Cardinal of Winchester led the entire English delegation out of Arras without having reached any agreement with the French. . . . And they suspected what in fact was to happen soon afterwards, that is to say that King Charles and the Duke of Burgundy were growing cordial toward each other. For they perceived even before their departure that those two parties had a great liking for one another. Soon after the departure of the English ambassadors from the town of Arras to return to England the two other parties who had stayed at Arras, that is the French and the Burgundians, met together again in conference at the accustomed place, where they had a great discussion together about various matters and they agreed to make a final peace between King Charles on the one hand and Duke Philip of Burgundy on the other, and in order to reach this fines and great reparations were made and promised to Duke Philip of Burgundy for the death of Duke John his father, by King Charles of France. This peace was made to the very great displeasure of the King of England and of all his prelates, princes, and barons, and of all the English council, especially the Cardinal of Winchester. Finally, peace was made between the two princes and published throughout the realm of France. This occasioned much thankfulness, and all kinds of people gave thanks and praise for it to Our Lord Jesus Christ."

tum by taking Lagny. On August 10, after a hot, brutal battle, he was forced to abandon the attempt. Many men-at-arms had died, not of wounds, but of heatstroke. Bedford's exertions at Lagny probably damaged his health permanently.

In November, Anne of Burgundy died—"a political disaster," according to Seward.[129] Only Anne had been able to keep the alliance between Bedford and Burgundy intact. The chronicler Jean de Wavrin feared "that because of this unhappy event the love and alliance which had existed for a long time between her husband and Duke Philip of Burgundy, who had loved her very dearly, would grow somewhat cold."[130] Sure enough, Philip, afraid the English and French would form an alliance against him, began exploring a settlement of his old feud with Charles.

Bedford returned to England in 1433 to answer charges in Parliament that he was incompetent. He successfully defended himself and won the praise of Parliament. He returned to France in 1434 in time to put down a rebellion in Normandy, whose people had suffered greatly. Like the *routiers* of the previous century, heavily armed bands plundered the countryside. Because of their practice of taking everything from their victims, even their shirts, they were known as *écorcheurs,* or "skinners." Sometimes they actually skinned their victims, as well.

In 1435 Philip of Burgundy was ready to abandon the English, and his lawyers provided him with an excuse. The Treaty of Troyes, his lawyers explained, provided that Charles VI would pass the French crown to Henry V of England and to his heirs. Since Henry had died before Charles, they said, it could not legally pass to Henry's son.

The Treaty of Arras

The French, Burgundians, and English agreed to meet at Arras in the summer to reach a general settlement. The conference began in August. Bedford was now seriously ill in Rouen, so Beaufort was chief negotiator for the English. He refused to discuss giving up either the English claim to the French throne or the sovereignty of Normandy. After six weeks of arguing there was no agreement, and Beaufort broke off the talks.

A week after the talks ended, Bedford died. He had come close to success in making Henry VI king of all France. He had failed, but his influence had been so great and the structure he had built so strong that it would last another two decades. He was "noble in birth and worth; wise, liberal, feared, and loved."[131]

Talks soon resumed without the English, and on September 20 Philip of Burgundy and Charles VI signed the Treaty of Arras. Charles granted Philip new lands and vowed to build a monument to the murdered duke, John the Fearless. He also promised to have a representative apologize for the murder, in his name and on his knees, before Duke Philip—"a hard blow to the vanity of the King of France."[132] Charles, however, got what he most wanted from Burgundy: recognition as king of all France.

Chapter

9 The Triumph of France

The Treaty of Arras, in which Philip of Burgundy acknowledged Charles VII as king of France, shocked England. The English considered Philip a traitor. London mobs hunted down and killed Burgundian merchants. Henry VI wept when he received a letter from Philip that failed to acknowledge him as king of France. In France the Treaty of Arras touched off uprisings throughout the country against English strongholds. Several towns in Normandy were captured by the French, including Harfleur.

In February 1436 Arthur de Richemont, Charles's chief commander, blockaded Paris with an army of five thousand men. On April 13 the Parisians opened the gates to a force led by Jean Dunois. The English were forced to retreat to the city's chief fortress. After negotiations they were allowed to leave. The anonymous Parisian bourgeois wrote, "No one was ever jeered at and booed as they were."[133]

In July Philip of Burgundy began a siege of English-owned Calais. The duke of Gloucester landed with an army in August,

French troops attack Paris in 1436 and take it back from the English.

Charles VII's triumphal entry into Paris in 1437 was cheered by its inhabitants.

chased off Philip's troops, and led a *chevauchée* into Flanders. Several cities in Flanders revolted against Philip, who eventually signed a truce with England in 1438. From this time on, he did not play an active part in the war.

English Threaten Paris

Sir John Talbot had succeeded Bedford as the principal English commander. He repulsed an attack on Rouen in 1436 and the next year captured Pontoise, only twelve miles from Paris. His exploits made Paris so dangerous that, after Charles VII made his triumphal entry into his capital in 1437, he stayed only three weeks. This entry, nevertheless, made an impression on the people of Paris, as described by the bourgeois writer:

> He arrived in Paris on the day after Martinmas [feast day of Saint Martin]

1437, and was welcomed as magnificently as if he had been God. He came in through the Porte St. Denis fully armed in shining armor, together with the Dauphin [Charles's son Louis], a boy about ten years old. . . . When he had got about as far as the Hôtel-Dieu, the doors of the church of Notre Dame were closed and the Bishop of Paris brought a book to the King upon which he swore as King that he would faithfully and loyally keep all that a good king should. . . . He stayed the night at the Palais [palace]. There were great celebrations that night, pots and pans being thumped, bonfires in the middle of the streets, eating, drinking, dancing, various instruments playing. Thus the King came to Paris, as is here described.[134]

Charles was far less popular with the leading nobles. He was cautious and, instead of following the capture of Paris

The English Are Expelled from Paris

For almost thirty years Paris was occupied by either the Burgundians or the English. Jean de Wavrin described how the English were finally expelled in 1436. The passage is found in A. R. Myers's English Historical Documents:

"The lord of L'Isle Adam called forward the French army, which arrived at the gates of Paris. He treated [negotiated] with the Parisians and showed them a deed of amnesty [forgiveness] from King Charles. They were therefore persuaded to return to the obedience of their natural lord, especially as the English were becoming so enfeebled. And so ladders were set up against the wall, and by them the lord of L'Isle Adam climbed up and with him climbed up [Jean Dunois]. With them gathered a very great number of [common people] of this noble city, and began to cry excitedly in great tumult, 'Long Live King Charles and the noble Duke of Burgundy!' and soon afterward caused the gates to be opened, by which came in quickly the Constable of France and with him several great lords of his company and their men at arms. All of them hastened to the Bastille of St. Anthony where the English had retreated for fear of their danger. There they were barricaded by the French, and the goods they had left in the town were pillaged. Citizens of the English party were made prisoner and new officers were appointed. The English in the Bastille made terms for surrender and were allowed to go to Rouen. They departed amidst the hooting and the mockery of the Parisians."

with an all-out attack, did nothing. The nobles also were jealous of the power of Richemont. In 1440 a group that included the dukes of Alençon, Bourbon, and Brittany—and even Charles VII's son Louis, the new dauphin—attempted to remove Charles from the throne but failed.

The fighting continued, some towns being taken by first one side, then the other. The French besieged Pontoise in June 1441, but Talbot marched to its rescue. Yet, when Talbot returned to Normandy in September, Charles began the siege again. This time he had with him Jean Bureau, a master of gunnery. Bureau's cannons quickly knocked down part of the city walls. Pontoise surrendered, and after more than twenty years, the area around Paris was now totally French.

Henry VI's French Marriage

King Henry VI, now eighteen, was dominated by Beaufort. When Beaufort retired in 1444, his place was taken by the earl of Suffolk, who, like Beaufort, wanted peace. Suffolk met with the French at Tours to discuss a truce. Under its terms there would be a truce of two years, the county of Le Maine would be surrendered to France, and Henry VI would marry Margaret of Anjou, Charles's sixteen-year-old niece. Suffolk knew how unpopular the surrender of Le Maine

Margaret of Anjou, the niece of Charles VII, married King Henry VI of England in 1445. The English hated her because she was loyal to France.

would be in England and managed to keep that part of the bargain a secret.

Henry and Margaret were married in 1445, and the young girl quickly gained complete control over her weak, feeble-minded husband. She was "ambitious, active, and intense. . . . French at heart, she stood for peace and did nothing to wrest from the Valois the provinces recently lost by England."[135] The people of England knew her contempt for them and hated her bitterly.

Margaret convinced Henry in 1445 to honor the promise to surrender Le Maine, which would not occur for three years. Word of the secret leaked out, however, and Suffolk's opponents—mainly Gloucester and Richard, duke of York—called for his removal from office. But Suffolk managed to silence the opposition. In February 1447 Gloucester was arrested and died shortly afterward, perhaps murdered. Richard of York, next in line for the English throne since Henry had no children, was sent to Ireland to keep him out of the way.

The Change in Charles VII

After Le Maine was surrendered to the French in 1448, Charles VII felt strong enough to launch an attack on Normandy. Charles was now a different person from the indecisive dauphin he had been in the 1420s. Seward wrote:

> Above all the French King himself had at last matured. His natural astuteness and flexibility had been reinforced by an implacable determination. He became a good organizer and a subtle politician, ruthless

and unscrupulous, with a nice talent for espionage and bribery. [136]

He had brought the leading nobles in line by putting down the rebellion of 1440. He had reformed the army, making it Europe's first standing army, paid regularly in peacetime as well as in wartime. He recognized the value of gunnery and spent much money having Jean Bureau modernize the cannon.

In July 1449 the French attacked Normandy from three sides, and many towns fell to them. On October 16 they assaulted Rouen but were repelled by Talbot. The French prepared for a siege, but the people of Rouen, remembering how they had suffered in 1418, rioted and opened the gates to the French. The English took refuge in a castle and eventually were allowed to retreat, leaving Talbot as a hostage.

The Battle of Fromigny

England was alarmed by the fall of Rouen and sent troops, but only four thousand, to Normandy under Thomas Kyriell. He landed at Cherbourg on March 15, 1450, and marched toward Bayeux, which was besieged by the French. He was intercepted near the village of Fromigny by the count of Clermont on April 15.

The English took up defensive positions, exactly the same as at Crécy, Poitiers, and Agincourt, but the French refused to charge. Instead, they brought up cannons and began firing, eventually forcing the English to charge. The battle was in doubt until twelve hundred fresh French troops, led by Richemont, attacked Kyriell from behind. The English were routed and Kyriell was taken prisoner.

In 1451 French troops invade and conquer English-ruled Guyenne in southern France.

The Battle of Fromigny, "the first major battle lost by the English since Bannockburn in 1314,"[137] sealed the fate of Normandy. In June Caen fell to the French. In July the town of Falaise surrendered to Charles, part of the bargain being the freedom of Talbot. Cherbourg came last. Bureau's cannons shelled the city for weeks. Enguerrand de Monstrelet wrote, "The town received such a heavy battering from cannons and bombards [bombs of large stones] that the like had never been seen before."[138] Cherbourg surrendered on August 12, 1450, and Normandy was French once more after thirty years of occupation.

The loss of Normandy "shocked all England."[139] Parliament accused Suffolk of treason. He tried to escape to Calais but was caught at sea. On May 2, possibly on orders from the duke of York, he was made to stretch his neck over the side of a small boat. It took six strokes from a rusty sword to hack off his head.

The Invasion of Guyenne

In France Charles quickly turned his attention to Guyenne. Except for one invasion in 1438, Guyenne had been relatively peaceful. It was different from Normandy: "Guyenne had belonged to the Plantagenets for 300 years, not a mere thirty."[140]

The French invaded late in 1450 but had little success. They had better luck in 1451. With Jean Dunois leading the army and Jean Bureau battering the walls with his artillery, the French captured the capital, Bordeaux, on June 30. The last city in Guyenne, Bayonne, fell on August 20.

John Talbot was England's greatest military leader at the end of the Hundred Years' War.

The people of Guyenne were highly independent and soon grew to hate the harsh rule of the French. In 1452 they sent delegates to London and promised to help throw the French out if England would send an army. The English turned to Talbot to lead the expedition. He sailed in October 1452 and surprised the French by landing in Guyenne instead of in Normandy. The people of Guyenne did as they had promised. The gates of Bordeaux were opened to the English on October 21. Soon, all the western half of the county was in English hands once more.

Charles counterattacked in the spring of 1453. Three French armies invaded from different directions, all heading for Bordeaux. Talbot knew his only chance was to defeat one army at a time. In July he marched to meet the army besieging the town of Castillon.

The Battle of Castillon

Jean Bureau had built at Castillon what was then relatively new in warfare, a fortified artillery park. It consisted of an earthen wall, strengthened by tree trunks. Deep trenches, through which cannons could be moved into position, ran toward the town.

Talbot arrived at Castillon on July 17. He was accompanied by only thirteen hundred mounted men. While Talbot was

The Death of Talbot

England's greatest soldier during the last years of the war was Sir John Talbot. This account of his death at the Battle of Castillon, the war's final battle, is from Jean Chartier's Chronique Française du Roi de Charles VII *and is found in A. R. Myers's* English Historical Documents:

"Now Talbot and his company began to arrive in great force, and came up close to the barrier which protected the camp. But they found there a formidable array of valiant men, very expert in warfare. They showed themselves courageous and bold, and greeted the English bravely and with spirit, and sturdily pushed them back and made them retreat. This astonished [the English] very much, in view of the message [that the French were retreating] they had received from the defenders of the town. In this encounter Talbot was mounted on a little hackney [horse] because he was a very old man, but he made all those of his company who had come on horseback fight on foot. Then began a great and terrible assault, with acts of great bravery on both sides, hand to hand fighting, and marvelous struggles...and many valiant blows.... As soon as [French] reinforcements arrived, they did so well, with the aid of God and by their prowess, that the English turned at last their backs, and were put to flight and defeated.... And all their banners were thrown down, and they left many dead on the field; in particular Talbot's hackney was struck by a shot from a culverine [a type of gun], so that it fell at once to the ground quite dead; and at the same time Talbot, his master, was thrown under it, and was at once killed by some archers. And thus died this famous and renowned English leader, who for so long had been reputed to be one of the most formidable scourges of the French, and one of their most sworn enemies, and had seemed to be the dread and terror of France."

The End of the War

The end of the Hundred Years' War came with the surrender of Bordeaux on October 19, 1453. This description by Jean Chartier is found in English Historical Documents:

"But at last when the said English and Gascons [citizens of Guyenne] saw themselves oppressed and overwhelmed, and were running short of food, they were very amazed for they saw all the strong places and fortresses of the surrounding countryside reduced by force of arms, and put in full and entire obedience to the King of France. They asked for favourable terms. The king agreed to this for two reasons; first, he was ready to render good for evil; secondly, he took account of the great mortality [death rate] in his camp so that in order to get a change of air, he was ready to make an agreement with the English in the following form. . . . The town and city of Bordeaux was to be restored and given up to the King of France, and all the inhabitants would remain his true and obedient subjects, and would take an oath never to rebel again or rise against the crown of France, and to recognize and affirm that the King of France was their sovereign lord. Then the English had permission to leave by means of their ships either for England or Calais, as should seem best to them."

waiting for the rest, a messenger came from the town to report that the French were retreating. The townspeople had actually seen only the dust raised by a few horses. Talbot did not want the French to escape and attacked the artillery park with what men he had.

As the English charged up the earthen wall, the French guns opened fire, killing as many as six men with each shot. Then, about a thousand mounted soldiers appeared suddenly and attacked the English from the left. The English began to retreat. Talbot tried to rally them but was pinned down when his horse was killed by a gunshot. A French archer killed the great English commander with an axe as he lay helplessly on the ground. Only a few English survived.

Without English troops Guyenne could not hold out long against Charles. At last only Bordeaux was left, and it surrendered on October 19. A grateful Charles made Jean Bureau mayor of Bordeaux for life.

Guyenne was French once more after three centuries. Of the huge Angevin Empire, only Calais remained in English hands. There was no truce, no treaty. Neither country knew it at the time, but the Hundred Years' War was over.

Epilogue

Importance of the Hundred Years' War

The war had affected everyone from nobles to peasants. Thousands fought and died; millions more were heavily taxed to pay for it. And, although the war had ended, its impact continued long after the guns fell silent and the swords rusted.

What had been gained or lost? In terms of territory, the French won. Calais was still English, but the French had regained wealthy Guyenne. Yet, this was a small reward. Perroy wrote:

> The price of victory often withers its fruits in advance. For France as a whole the Hundred Years War had been an immense trial, from which [it] emerged weakened and worn and incapable for centuries of resuming [its] former position. Gone was the peaceful hegemony [power] which the last Capetians, though with limited resources, had exercised over a Europe even less well equipped. . . . All the fighting, all the plundering, all the epidemics had greatly reduced both the population and its capacity for production.[141]

The Making of Two Nations

The long-term effect of the Hundred Years' War, however, was that both France and England became nations with strong central governments instead of feudal kingdoms. As the great nobles of France were killed or forced to pay huge ransoms,

English soldiers battle each other during England's War of the Roses that followed the Hundred Years' War. The War of the Roses killed off much of England's nobility, thus strengthening the monarchy.

The end of the Hundred Years' War also signalled the end of feudalism.

the royal government grew more powerful. The huge amounts of money needed for the war led to permanent forms of taxation and more efficient government. In France, Perroy wrote, "this progress toward absolute monarchy was a legacy of the war with England, which had shown the need of strong and effective power."[142]

In England the same thing happened, only later. Henry VI, who inherited, if only briefly, the throne of his grandfather, Charles VI, inherited his madness, as well. His mind gave way in 1453. The resulting struggle for power between Henry's wife, Margaret of Anjou, and his cousin, the duke of York, brought about the War of the Roses. This thirty-year struggle caused the deaths of so many of the English nobility that their dominance over the country was weakened, leading to an increase in the power of the monarchy. The War of the Roses has thus been called "a blessing in disguise"[143] for England.

The End of Feudalism

The war thus put an end to feudalism. The old system could not survive in a more modern system of national government. English historian George M. Trevelyan wrote:

> We [the English] persisted so long in this disastrous enterprise 'till our own well-ordered medieval society was ruined, and 'till we had twice goaded the French themselves . . . to be conscious of their national identity and to change the purely feudal tactics and spirit of their armies. The Hundred Years' War was the diplomatic and military aspect of the period of transition from the feudal to the national, from the Middle Ages to the Renaissance.[144]

The growing power of the kings was not the only contribution of the war toward English and French patriotism. People on each side of the channel united against common enemies. Decades of suffering led the French to hate the English, whom they called "Godons" or "God-damns."

The war brought England a new respect throughout Europe. Jean le Bel wrote, "When the noble Edward [III] first gained England in his youth, nobody thought much of the English, nobody spoke of their prowess or courage. . . . Now, in the time of the noble Edward, who has often put them to the test, they are the finest and most daring warriors known to man."[145] From this time on the English began to look with contempt on all foreigners. This feeling of superiority continued into future centuries, when the British Empire had colonies all over the world.

A Legacy of Hatred

The mutual hatred of the French and English was also to prove harmful. Fighting between the nations by no means stopped in 1453. They clashed many times over the next four hundred years, including a long and bloody war between England and Napoleon Bonaparte. Only in our own cen-

---

Anger at the Pope

Some of the French-born popes in Avignon openly supported France during the Hundred Years' War. This parliamentary petition of 1376 shows how the war turned the English against the pope. It is found in English Historical Documents:

"The court of Rome [the papacy], which ought to be the fountain, root, and source of holiness and destruction of covetousness . . . and other sins, has so subtly in the course of time attracted to itself the collation [group] of bishoprics, dignities, prebendaries, and other benefices [all officials] of Holy Church in England, from which the tax amounts to more than five times the tax of all the profits which belong to the king each year from his whole realm. . . . And when a bishop has his bulls [being named bishop], he is so much indebted to the court of Rome for the tax and other payments and costs, that he has to sell the woods of his bishopric, to borrow from his friends, to have an aid [payment] from his poor tenants, and to gain a subsidy [payment] from the clergy. And all goes in destruction of Holy Church and the kingdom of England. . . . Also let it be considered how law and reason and good faith require that what is given to Holy Church out of devotion should be spent for the honour of God, according to the devotion and intent of the donor, and not spent outside the realm on our enemies."

Innovations in Warfare

"And these [soldiers] were paid each month, so that they did not dare nor venture during this war and conquest of Normandy to take any of the people of that countryside prisoners, nor to take or ransom any beast whatever it was, whether they were in the obedience of the English or of their own side; nor to seize any victuals [food supplies] wherever they were, without paying for them, except only from the English or their adherents, in which case they could take the victuals lawfully. . . . Just as important was the provision that the king had made in his artillery for warfare and he had a very great number of great bombards, great cannons, veuglaires, serpentines, crapaudins, culverins, and ribaudquins [all various kinds of artillery], so that never in the memory of man did a Christian king have such a numerous artillery at one time, nor so well furnished with powder, shot, and all other things necessary to approach and take towns and castles. . . . And the organizers of this artillery were Master Jean Bureau, treasurer of France, and Gaspard Bureau, his brother, who during these wars have suffered great pains and were found in many perils, for they have done well their best and have acquitted themselves well of their duty, with satisfaction to all."

tury, as a result of World War I and World War II, have France and England become true allies.

More than one hundred years of almost constant warfare brought about military changes and improvements. The armored horseman had for centuries been the ultimate weapon, until he came up against the longbow. Guns were even more effective than the longbow, once they were made relatively efficient and could be fired without too much danger of exploding.

Edward III had cannons at Crécy, but they "were seldom lethal, except to those firing them."[146] Charles VII of France realized the importance of artillery, and Jean Bureau's guns made the difference in the last years of the war.

The development of archery and gunnery, however, had an importance far beyond the battlefield. The ability of a man to pay for armor and horses made him a "gentleman" and distinguished him from the common man. McKisack wrote that, with Crécy, "the day of the feudal horseman was almost over. . . . This was an unpalatable truth for the heroes of chivalry to digest."[147] The bow and the gun brought those who fired them closer in the social order to the men-at-arms. Together with the Black Death, which gave the ordinary people economic power, the military might of the common soldier contributed to an unwillingness to accept traditional low status. The Jacquerie and the Peasants' Revolt, "a sign of independence and self-respect in the medieval peasants,"[148] were the direct ancestors of the American and French revolutions.

The other chief military development was the formation of the standing army. First, it meant that in times of peace, the country was not filled with out-of-work soldiers, who frequently became outlaws. Second, it gave the king a permanent armed force, something useful for dealing with rebellious nobles.

Even religion was affected, particularly in England. For much of the war the Catholic popes lived in France. This made the papacy increasingly unpopular with the English, who had a "self-righteous hatred of the pope at Avignon."[149] An influential fourteenth-century priest, John Wycliffe, preached against the authority of the pope and had a large following who called themselves Lollards. All this made it far easier for England, in the 1530s, to break from the Catholic church.

The Effect on Language

The war changed the language of England. Previously the nobility spoke Norman French. English was considered fit only for the lower classes. By the time of the Battle of Poitiers, French was "the enemy language."[150] It is not certain whether Edward III could even speak English. Yet, his great-grandson, Henry V, insisted that negotiations be done in Latin rather than French, which he claimed neither he nor

John Wycliffe, a fourteenth-century English priest, translated the Bible into English and opposed the pope's spiritual authority.

William Shakespeare summed up the feelings of the patriotism of his countrymen with this speech by John of Gaunt in Richard II, *as printed in* The Living Shakespeare:

This royal throne of kings, this scepter'd isle,
This earth of majesty, this seat of Mars,
This other Eden, demi-paradise,
This fortress built by Nature for herself
Against infection and the hand of war,
This happy breed of men, this little world,
This precious stone set in the silver sea,
Which serves it in the office of a wall
Or as a moat defensive to a house,
Against the envy of less happier lands,
This blessed plot, this earth, this realm, this England.

his ambassadors "could write properly, understand, or speak."[151]

When the upper classes began to speak English, it meant that books, which only they could afford, would be written in that language. The war thus led to "the whole development of English national life and letters as something other than a northern offshoot of French culture. Some may regard this revolution as more important than Magna Carta or the Declaration of Independence."[152]

A Bridge to the Present

The Hundred Years' War ended the old ways more than it began the new. Europe could never return to what it was before

1337. The war destroyed feudalism and prepared the way for the Renaissance, the rebirth of learning that had already begun in Italy. David Douglas wrote:

> After the Hundred Years War neither the French nor English ever thought about each other in quite the same way as they had done before it began, and never again were they to be conscious in quite the former manner as belonging to the same overriding political system. Feudalism as a cohesive force between and within the two peoples had been destroyed. Passing also were those ideas of political and social solidarity among the western peoples which the men of an earlier generation had respected though never realized. A new wind was beginning to blow from across the Alps.[153]

Appendix 1

Royal Succession
The Capetian and Valois Kings of France
and the Dukes of Burgundy

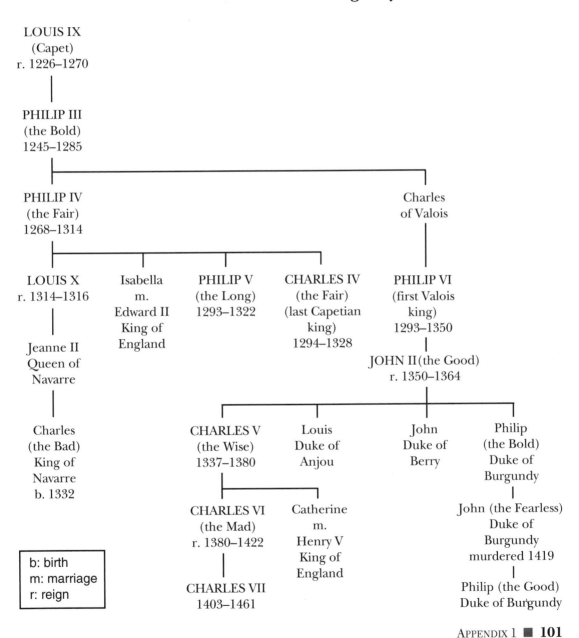

Appendix 2

The Kings of England

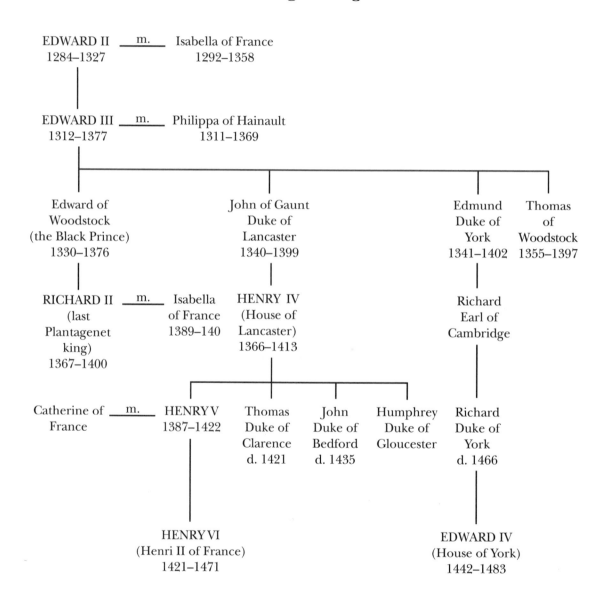

EDWARD II ___m.___ Isabella of France
1284–1327   1292–1358

EDWARD III ___m.___ Philippa of Hainault
1312–1377   1311–1369

Edward of Woodstock (the Black Prince) 1330–1376

John of Gaunt Duke of Lancaster 1340–1399

Edmund Duke of York 1341–1402

Thomas of Woodstock 1355–1397

RICHARD II (last Plantagenet king) 1367–1400 ___m.___ Isabella of France 1389–140

HENRY IV (House of Lancaster) 1366–1413

Richard Earl of Cambridge

Catherine of France ___m.___ HENRY V 1387–1422

Thomas Duke of Clarence d. 1421

John Duke of Bedford d. 1435

Humphrey Duke of Gloucester

Richard Duke of York d. 1466

HENRY VI (Henri II of France) 1421–1471

EDWARD IV (House of York) 1442–1483

m: marriage
d: died

Notes

Introduction: The Endless War

1. David Douglas, in introduction to Edouard Perroy, *The Hundred Years War*. W. B. Wells, translator. London: Eyre and Spotteswoode, 1959.
2. Perroy, *The Hundred Years War*.

Chapter 1: Plantagenet and Valois

3. Thomas Gray, quoted in Michael Packe, *King Edward III*. London: Ark Paperbacks, 1985.
4. Desmond Seward, *The Hundred Years War: The English in France, 1337–1453*. New York: Atheneum, 1978.
5. Jean Froissart, *Froissart's Chronicles*. John Jolife, translator. New York: Modern Library, 1967.
6. Seward, *The Hundred Years War*.
7. Quoted in May McKisack, *The Fourteenth Century: 1307–1399*. Clarendon, England: Oxford Press, 1959.
8. Jean le Bel, quoted in Seward, *The Hundred Years War*.
9. Perroy, *The Hundred Years War*.
10. McKisack, *The Fourteenth Century*.
11. Quoted in Perroy, *The Hundred Years War*.
12. Froissart, *Froissart's Chronicles*.
13. Froissart, *Froissart's Chronicles*.
14. Thomas Rymer, *Foedora*, in *English Historical Documents: 1327–1485*. A. R. Myers, editor. New York: Oxford University Press, 1969.
15. Quoted in Perroy, *The Hundred Years War*.
16. Packe, *King Edward III*.

Chapter 2: France and England

17. Perroy, *The Hundred Years War*.
18. Froissart, quoted in Kenneth Fowler, *The Age of Plantagenet and Valois*. New York: G. P. Putnam's Sons, 1967.

19. Matthew Paris, quoted in Seward, *The Hundred Years War*.
20. Froissart, *Froissart's Chronicles*.
21. Fowler, *The Age of Plantagenet and Valois*.
22. Perroy, *The Hundred Years War*.
23. Fowler, *The Age of Plantagenet and Valois*.
24. Fowler, *The Age of Plantagenet and Valois*.
25. Fowler, *The Age of Plantagenet and Valois*.
26. George Holmes, *The Later Middle Ages: 1272–1485*. New York: W. W. Norton, 1962.
27. McKisack, *The Fourteenth Century*.
28. Perroy, *The Hundred Years War*.
29. Packe, *King Edward III*.
30. Perroy, *The Hundred Years War*.
31. McKisack, *The Fourteenth Century*.
32. Perroy, *The Hundred Years War*.

Chapter 3: Sluys, Crécy, and Calais

33. Quoted in Packe, *King Edward III*.
34. Froissart, *Froissart's Chronicles*.
35. Seward, *The Hundred Years War*.
36. Thomas Walsingham, quoted in James MacKinnon, *The History of Edward the Third*. 1900. Reprint. Totowa, NJ: Rowman and Littlefield, 1974.
37. Packe, *King Edward III*.
38. Froissart, *Froissart's Chronicles*.
39. Froissart, *Froissart's Chronicles*.
40. Bel, quoted in Seward, *The Hundred Years War*.
41. Froissart, *Froissart's Chronicles*.
42. Froissart, *Froissart's Chronicles*.
43. Froissart, *Froissart's Chronicles*.
44. Seward, *The Hundred Years War*.
45. Froissart, *Froissart's Chronicles*.
46. Seward, *The Hundred Years War*.

47. Robert of Avesbury, *Chronicle*, quoted in Packe, *King Edward III*.

48. Froissart, *Froissart's Chronicles*.

49. Quoted in Perroy, *The Hundred Years War*.

Chapter 4: The Black Death, the Black Prince, and Poitiers

50. Philip Ziegler, *The Black Death*. New York: Harper and Row, 1969.

51. Ziegler, *The Black Death*.

52. Quoted in Ziegler, *The Black Death*.

53. Perroy, *The Hundred Years War*.

54. MacKinnon, *The History of Edward the Third*.

55. Fowler, *The Age of Plantagenet and Valois*.

56. Walsingham, quoted in Seward, *The Hundred Years War*.

57. John Harvey, *The Black Prince and His Age*. Totowa, NJ: Rowman and Littlefield, 1976.

58. Harvey, *The Black Prince*.

59. Seward, *The Hundred Years War*.

60. Perroy, *The Hundred Years War*.

61. Geoffrey le Baker, *Chronicle*, in Myers, *English Historical Documents*.

62. Baker, *Chronicle*, in Myers, *English Historical Documents*.

63. Baker, *Chronicle*, in Myers, *English Historical Documents*.

64. Baker, *Chronicle*, in Myers, *English Historical Documents*.

65. Froissart, *Froissart's Chronicles*.

66. Harvey, *The Black Prince*.

67. Froissart, quoted in Seward, *The Hundred Years War*.

68. Jean de Venette, *Chronicle*, in Myers, *English Historical Documents*.

69. Froissart, *Froissart's Chronicles*.

70. Perroy, *The Hundred Years War*.

71. Quoted in Seward, *The Hundred Years War*.

72. Perroy, *The Hundred Years War*.

73. Perroy, *The Hundred Years War*.

Chapter 5: Charles the Wise

74. Perroy, *The Hundred Years War*.

75. Perroy, *The Hundred Years War*.

76. Seward, *The Hundred Years War*.

77. Harvey, *The Black Prince*.

78. Perroy, *The Hundred Years War*.

79. Froissart, *Froissart's Chronicles*.

80. Froissart, *Froissart's Chronicles*.

81. Froissart, *Froissart's Chronicles*.

82. Perroy, *The Hundred Years War*.

83. Perroy, *The Hundred Years War*.

84. McKisack, *The Fourteenth Century*.

85. Perroy, *The Hundred Years War*.

Chapter 6: A Lengthy Interlude

86. Maurice Collins, *The Hurling Time*. London: Faber and Faber, 1958.

87. Quoted in Seward, *The Hundred Years War*.

88. Quoted in McKisack, *The Fourteenth Century*.

89. Perroy, *The Hundred Years War*.

90. Perroy, *The Hundred Years War*.

91. Rymer, quoted in McKisack, *The Fourteenth Century*.

92. Froissart, *Froissart's Chronicles*.

93. McKisack, *The Fourteenth Century*.

94. Perroy, *The Hundred Years War*.

95. Quoted in Seward, *The Hundred Years War*.

Chapter 7: Henry V and Agincourt

96. William Stubbs, quoted in Harold Hutchison, *King Henry V*. New York: Dorset Press, 1967.

97. R. B. Mowat, quoted in Hutchison, *King Henry V*.

98. Perroy, *The Hundred Years War*.

99. From *Henrici Quinti Angliae Regis Gesta (Life of Henry the Fifth, King of England)*, in Myers, *English Historical Documents*.

100. E. Halle, quoted in Hutchison, *King Henry V*.

101. Seward, *The Hundred Years War.*

102. Hutchison, *King Henry V.*

103. Perroy, *The Hundred Years War.*

104. Janet Shirley, translator, *Journal d'un Bourgeois de Paris (Diary of a Bourgeois of Paris).* Clarendon, England: Oxford Press, 1968.

105. John Page, *The Siege of Rouen,* appendix in Hutchison, *King Henry V.*

106. Page, in Hutchison, *King Henry V.*

107. Jean Juvenal des Ursin, *Historie de Charles VI (History of Charles VI),* in Myers, *English Historical Documents.*

108. Hutchison, *King Henry V.*

109. Seward, *The Hundred Years War.*

110. Enguerrand de Monstrelet, quoted in Hutchison, *King Henry V.*

111. Shirley, *Journal d'un Bourgeois de Paris.*

112. Monstrelet, quoted in Hutchison, *King Henry V.*

Chapter 8: The Duke, the Dauphin, and the Maid

113. Perroy, *The Hundred Years War.*

114. Pierre de Fenin, quoted by M. G. A. Vale in *Charles VII.* Berkeley: University of California Press, 1974.

115. Seward, *The Hundred Years War.*

116. Seward, *The Hundred Years War.*

117. Perroy, *The Hundred Years War.*

118. Quoted in Seward, *The Hundred Years War.*

119. Perroy, *The Hundred Years War.*

120. Quoted in Vale, *Charles VII.*

121. Jules Quicherat, quoted in Edward Lucie-Smith, *Joan of Arc.* New York: W. W. Norton Company Inc., 1976.

122. Quicherat, quoted in Lucie-Smith, *Joan of Arc.*

123. Pierre Tisset and Yvonne Lanhers, quoted in Lucie-Smith, *Joan of Arc.*

124. Perroy, *The Hundred Years War.*

125. Quicherat, quoted in Lucie-Smith, *Joan of Arc.*

126. Monstrelet, quoted in Seward, *The Hundred Years War.*

127. Shirley, *Journal d'un Bourgeois de Paris.*

128. Perroy, *The Hundred Years War.*

129. Seward, *The Hundred Years War.*

130. Jean de Wavrin, quoted in Seward, *The Hundred Years War.*

131. Shirley, *Journal d'un Bourgeois de Paris.*

132. Perroy, *The Hundred Years War.*

Chapter 9: The Triumph of France

133. Shirley, *Journal d'un Bourgeois de Paris.*

134. Shirley, *Journal d'un Bourgeois de Paris.*

135. Perroy, *The Hundred Years War.*

136. Seward, *The Hundred Years War.*

137. Seward, *The Hundred Years War.*

138. Quoted in Seward, *The Hundred Years War.*

139. Seward, *The Hundred Years War.*

140. Seward, *The Hundred Years War.*

Epilogue: Importance of the Hundred Years' War

141. Perroy, *The Hundred Years War.*

142. Perroy, *The Hundred Years War.*

143. George M. Trevelyan, *A Shortened History of England.* Harmondsworth, England: Penguin Books, 1962.

144. Trevelyan, *A Shortened History of England.*

145. Bel, quoted in McKisack, *The Fourteenth Century.*

146. Seward, *The Hundred Years War.*

147. McKisack, *The Fourteenth Century.*

148. Trevelyan, *A Shortened History of England.*

149. Seward, *The Hundred Years War.*

150. Trevelyan, *A Shortened History of England.*

151. Rymer, quoted in Hutchison, *King Henry V.*

152. Trevelyan, *A Shortened History of England.*

153. Douglas, in Perroy, *The Hundred Years War.*

For Further Reading

Richard W. Barber, *England in the Middle Ages*. New York: Seabury Press, 1976.

The Boy's Froissart. New York: Charles Scribner's Sons, 1907.

Janice Young Brooks, *Kings and Queens: The Plantagenets of England*. Nashville: Thomas Nelson, 1975.

Polly Schoyer Brooks, *Beyond the Myth: The Story of Joan of Arc*. New York: Lippincott, 1990.

Michael Byam, *Arms and Armor*. New York: Alfred A. Knopf, 1988.

Geoffrey Chaucer, *The Canterbury Tales*. Barbara Cohen, translator. New York: Lothrop, Lee, and Shepard, 1988.

John D. Clare, editor, *Fourteenth-Century Towns*. San Diego: Harcourt Brace Jovanovich, 1993.

John D. Clare, editor, *Knights in Armor*. San Diego: Harcourt Brace Jovanovich, 1992.

Arthur Conan Doyle, *The White Company*. New York: Dodd, Mead, 1962.

Dana Fradon, *Harold the Herald*. New York: Dutton's Children's Books, 1990.

Shirley Glubok, *Knights in Armor*. New York: Harper and Row, 1969.

Christopher Gravett, *Knight*. New York: Alfred A. Knopf, 1993.

David Macaulay, *Castle*. Boston: Houghton Mifflin, 1977.

Maurice Boutet de Monvielt, *Joan of Arc*. A. I. Du Pont Coleman, translator. New York: Viking, 1980.

Gwyneth Morgan, *Life in a Medieval Village*. New York: Cambridge University Press, 1975.

Scott O'Dell, *The Hawk That Dare Not Hunt by Day*. Boston: Houghton Mifflin, 1975.

James Rosenfield, *The Lion and the Lily*. New York: Dodd, 1972.

Catherine Storr, *Joan of Arc*. Milwaukee: Raintree Children's Books, 1985.

Sylvia Wright, *The Age of Chivalry*. New York: Warwick Press, 1988.

Works Consulted

Adam of Usk, *Chronicon Adae de Usk (Chronicle of Adam of Usk)*. Edward Maunde Thompson, translator. London: Henry Frowde, 1904. A chronicle covering the reign (1377–1399) of King Richard II of England, as written by a monk in his service.

Alfred H. Burne, *The Crécy War*. Westport, CT: Greenwood Press, 1976. A military history written by a professional soldier. Politics are passed over in favor of exhaustive detail of battles, chiefly Crécy and Poitiers.

Maurice Collins, *The Hurling Time*. London: Faber and Faber, 1958. Originally intended as a history of the Peasants' Revolt, this was expanded to include all of the Hundred Years' War from 1337 to 1381. Still, half the book deals only— and very well—with the years from 1377 to 1381.

Charles W. Eliot, editor, *Chronicle and Romance: Froissart, Malory, Holinshed*. New York: P. F. Collier and Son, 1910. Volume 35 of the Harvard Classics series, this contains Jean Froissart's chronicle as it describes Crécy, Poitiers, and the peasants' revolt. Old language makes this version harder to read than some others.

Kenneth Fowler, *The Age of Plantagenet and Valois*. New York: G. P. Putnam's Sons, 1967. An excellent summary made more appealing by the use of more than 150 photographs, drawings, and maps. Especially good is the long chapter on military customs, practices, and strategies on the part of the two sides, with plenty of detail on the armor and weapons of the time.

Jean Froissart, *Chronicles*. John Jolliffe, translator. New York: Modern Library, 1967. Severely abridged version of Froissart's history, although translation is very readable.

F. L. Ganshof, *Feudalism*. Philip Grierson, translator. New York: Harper and Row, 1961. Comprehensive examination of the feudal system with good concluding summary of the survival of feudal practices beyond the Middle Ages.

John Harvey, *The Black Prince and His Age*. Totowa, NJ: Rowman and Littlefield, 1976. Extremely detailed, yet readable, account of the life of Edward of Woodstock, the Black Prince. Does not hesitate to describe the less glorious aspects of the Black Prince.

George Holmes, *The Later Middle Ages: 1272–1485*. New York: W. W. Norton, 1962. Third volume in the Norton History of England series. Good summary of politics and events in England; fewer details on the war.

Harold F. Hutchison, *King Henry V*. New York: Dorset Press, 1967. Thorough examination of Henry's reign and of Henry as a man. A special bonus is the appendix, the account by English soldier John Page of the siege of Rouen.

E. F. Jacob, *The Fifteenth Century: 1399–1485*. Clarendon, England: Oxford Press, 1961. Sixth volume of the Oxford History of England series. Goes into great detail on events in England, less on the war in France.

Life of the Black Prince. Clarendon, England: Oxford Press, 1910. Epic poem of the life of the Black Prince, written by the anonymous herald of Sir John Chandos, who fought with the Black Prince, is given in the original French with English translation.

Edward Lucie-Smith, *Joan of Arc*. New York: W. W. Norton Company Inc., 1976. Outstanding, well-documented account of the life of Joan. Loaded with quotations from those who both served and scorned her. Good selection of photographs of places mentioned in the book.

James MacKinnon, *The History of Edward the Third*. 1900. Reprint. Totowa, NJ: Rowman and Littlefield, 1974. This biography is not as well documented or as well organized as later versions but is entertaining to read because of the quaint language and the author's frequent quotations from contemporary sources. Lack of index is a hindrance.

May McKisack, *The Fourteenth Century: 1307–1399*. Clarendon, England: Oxford Press, 1959. Fifth volume of the Oxford History of England series. No pictures and short on maps, but one of the best summaries of the era from the English point of view.

A. R. Myers, editor, *English Historical Documents: 1327–1485*. New York: Oxford University Press, 1969. The fourth in a multivolume series offering translations of all or part of documents written during the period. Includes everything from treaties to the cost of breakfast for the king's council.

Michael Packe, *King Edward III*. London: Ark Paperbacks, 1985. Comprehensive biography of Edward III, the last quarter of which was completed from Packe's notes by L. C. B. Seaman after the author's death in 1978. Genealogical charts are among the most understandable. Well written but somewhat difficult to read because of small print and lack of illustrations.

Sidney Painter, *Mediaeval Society*. Ithaca, NY: Cornell University Press, 1961. Although this covers the centuries preceding the Hundred Years' War, it contains a good discussion of the origins and organization of the feudal system.

Edouard Perroy, *The Hundred Years War*. W. B. Wells, translator. London: Eyre and Spot-teswoode, 1959. Widely considered the most comprehensive and authoritative book on the war. A Frenchman, Perroy tends to write from that point of view.

Desmond Seward, *The Hundred Years War: The English in France, 1337–1453*. New York: Atheneum, 1978. One of the most readable books on the war available. Sprightly, with many human interest angles. Covers the subject sufficiently for the casual reader but is short enough at under three hundred pages to avoid getting bogged down in too much detail.

William Shakespeare, *The Living Shakespeare*. Oscar James Campbell, editor. New York: Macmillan, 1958. A collection of twenty-two plays and the sonnets of Shakespeare, each accompanied by an essay detailing its history.

Janet Shirley, translator, *Journal d'un Bourgeois de Paris (Diary of a Bourgeois of Paris)*. Clarendon, England: Oxford Press, 1968. Fascinating account of life in France from 1405 to 1449 as written by an anonymous Parisian, probably a clergyman of the cathedral of Notre Dame.

George M. Trevelyan, *A Shortened History of England*. Harmondsworth, England: Penguin Books, 1962. Has been called the best single-volume history of England ever written, and with good reason. Marvelous writer gives all the whos, whens, and wheres along with the hows and whys.

M. G. A. Vale, *Charles VII*. Berkeley: University of California Press, 1974. Scholarly, yet sympathetic, biography of the man better known to history as Joan of Arc's dauphin rather than France's king.

Philip Ziegler, *The Black Death*. New York: Harper and Row, 1969. Year-by-year, country-by-country chronicle of the devastating plague of 1348–1351 in Europe. Especially fascinating is the account of medical knowledge at the time.

Index

Picture Credits

Cover photo by Giraudon/Art Resource, NY

Biblioteque Nationale, 26, 96

Giraudon/Art Resource, NY, 8

Historical Pictures/Stock Montage, 27, 28, 76, 80, 87, 90, 91, 92, 95, 99

Library of Congress, 9, 11, 12, 14, 16, 17, 18, 20, 22 (both), 29, 31, 33, 34, 35, 37, 38, 39, 41, 44, 46, 47 (both), 48, 49, 51, 53, 55, 57, 58, 59, 60 (both), 61, 62, 63, 64, 65, 66, 67, 68, 69, 71, 73, 74, 77, 78, 79, 81, 82, 83 (both), 84, 88

About the Author

William W. Lace is a native of Fort Worth, Texas. He holds a bachelor's degree from Texas Christian University, a master's from East Texas State University, and a doctorate from the University of North Texas. After working for newspapers in Baytown, Texas, and Fort Worth, he joined the University of Texas at Arlington as sports information director and later became the director of the news service. He is now director of college relations for the Tarrant County Junior College District in Fort Worth. He and his wife, Laura, live in Arlington and have two children. Lace has written two other biographies of baseball player Nolan Ryan and artist Michelangelo.